TO FEED THEIR HOPES

BOOKS BY JOHN SANFORD

The Water Wheel, 1933
The Old Man's Place, 1935
Seventy Times Seven, 1939
The People from Heaven, 1943
A Man Without Shoes, 1951
The Land That Touches Mine, 1953
Every Island Fled Away, 1964
The $300 Man, 1967
A More Goodly Country, 1975
Adirondack Stories, 1976
View From This Wilderness, 1977

JOHN SANFORD

To Feed Their Hopes

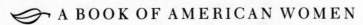 A BOOK OF AMERICAN WOMEN

Foreword by Annette K. Baxter

University of Illinois Press

URBANA CHICAGO LONDON

To Feed Their Hopes is the third part of a trilogy
on America, to be called *The Top of Pisgah*. The first
two parts have been published as:

> *A More Goodly Country* (1975)
> *View From This Wilderness* (1977)

Library of Congress Cataloging in Publication Data

Sanford, John B   1904–
   To feed their hopes.

   (*His* The top of Pisgah ; v. 3)
   1. Women—United States—Fiction. I. Title. II.
Series: Sanford, John B., 1904–   Top of Pisgah ;
v. 3.
PZ3.S2245Fe   [PS3537.A694]   813'.52   80–16505
ISBN 0–252–00804–9

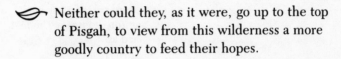 Neither could they, as it were, go up to the top of Pisgah, to view from this wilderness a more goodly country to feed their hopes.

William Bradford, *History of Plymouth Plantation*

CONTENTS

xi

FOREWORD

By some miracle, John Sanford—a man who loves America with passion—is passionately in love with facts. All of them, from the seemingly trivial to the shattering, apocalyptic ones, he loves for the hidden realities they may disguise and for the grace they often require of those who aspire to be equal to them.

In two previous volumes, on American history and American literature, Sanford has dealt with a vast assemblage of people, events, and experiences, always reaching for the telltale tremor, the revealing moment, the critical encounter. Unobserved, he steals up to the realities of emotion, of value, of human meaning. To him these are the authentic data of American life, and they enliven the finely wrought vignettes which compose each unit of his trilogy.

In *To Feed Their Hopes*, Sanford meets his most serious challenge. To write about women with the same intensity and confident authority he employs in his previous volumes could easily render him susceptible to the charge of assuming prerogatives that belong to women alone—an unfair imputation. While previous generations would hardly question the validity of his interpretations, they might have puzzled at his generosity in apportioning to women a third of his American trilogy. Today it is more likely that he will be commended for it. Nonetheless, there are those who will regard him with suspicion for daring to appropriate the rights to women's inner lives. How unfortunate if contemporary prejudices were to misjudge this wonderful book, crammed with the honest essence of so many female lives and so reflective of the author's devoted comprehension of both their misery and their glory.

Indeed, the book's purpose seems nothing less than a panoramic raising of the national consciousness with respect to women in American life. In his portraits of historical figures, Sanford seeks to penetrate the history behind the history, to comment on the feelings lurking around the facts, to question the public assertions that often mask the truths of women's lives. He intersperses his historical portraits with imaginative glosses on fictional characters: Lady Brett of *The Sun Also Rises* casts imprecations upon her creator; Zenobia of *Ethan Frome* counts her anguish after the climactic sledride. He offers fresh ruminations on familiar artifacts: *Model for a Bronze of Pomona* inspires a suggestive reassessment of New York's Pulitzer Fountain; *Hooded Figure* becomes the occasion for a searing recapitulation of the marriage of Clover and Henry Adams.

Sanford permits himself to scatter autobiographical reminiscences here and there. *A Nine-Page Letter* and *Someone Named Anne or Anna* serve to expose the author's sentiments in the way he has exposed those of others. Willing to share his own vulnerability with us, the author himself becomes a participant in the consciousness-raising process. He thereby witnesses to its importance as a preliminary to any larger historical comprehension, and he does so in a way that strengthens our grasp of the sensibility that plays upon his other subjects. Criticism and autobiography join in delineating the undercurrents of male-female interaction on a variety of levels—intellectual, psychological, sexual. Nothing and no one is spared, yet all emerge with their humanity confirmed and enhanced, the author's as well.

Sanford is aware of the tenuous nature of his enterprise, the borderline treading between fact and fancy. He does not violate the documented truths of history: Alice Roosevelt Longworth did indeed maliciously invite Lucy Mercer to her home with FDR. Neither does he shrink at the opportunity to imagine more than has been documented: in *The Wife of John Reed*, he shifts back and forth between the hypothesized last moments of Reed's wife and the medical certainties of the famous journalist's final illness. The pathos of Louise Bryant's life becomes manifest as its high point is equated with the Reed years. Sanford's choice of subject matter can illustrate his purpose as clearly as does his treatment. In *The Mistress of Citizen Kane*, he suggests the tragic formlessness of a woman's life; replicating its own cinematic image, the "liquefactive self" of Dorothy Comingore, the actress who played Kane's mistress, eludes definition and invites disintegration.

The women whom he remembers range from Little Eva and the young victims of Salem witches to Mary Baker Eddy, Wallis Warfield Simpson, and Bessie Smith. His canvas is broad, his sympathies tender, his insights keen. Sanford's view of women is of course a man's view, and it is valuable to us for being that. He demonstrates that it is possible for men, willing to equip themselves with knowledge and empathy, to scale the tangled emotional barbed wire between the sexes and cross over into understanding.

ANNETTE K. BAXTER
Barnard College

PREFACE
in the form of a memoir

In the autumn of 1914, you began the fifth grade of grammar school in a class conducted by a teacher named Grace Gibson. You'd known her earlier—she'd been an acquaintance of your mother's and a guest on occasion in your home—and when you reported to her on the first morning of the new term, she left a monitor in charge of the room and led you to her office across the corridor. There she sat you down and spoke to you of your mother, who'd died during the summer, scarcely a month before. You recall almost nothing that she said to you—you either resisted hearing it or expelled from your mind what you'd heard—but this much is certain, that you couldn't face her, that you never looked up from the floor.

You were ten at the time, going on eleven—the tender years, they're called, but how unyielding they really are! Your thought at ten, rising eleven, was that your mother's dying was a wrong she'd wrought on herself and, through herself, on you. As you saw it (where? down there on the floor?), her death was a willful act, one that had interfered with your life, modified it, deformed it, even—every family silence told you as much, every lowered voice, every shaken head—and when Miss Gibson said, "Do you realize what losing your mother means?" you tried to say Yes! Yes, I do!, but all you did was stare at the dust on the floor.

It was long in leaving you, that feeling of having been singled out as something less than equal: by some wrench of reasoning, you'd suffered a degradation, and you went among worthier classmates not unlike a trespasser. You had no friends there in that room, and to only a few were you drawn: a pretty girl, a manly sort of boy; it was a rare thing when Muriel spoke to you, or Esther, or Cornelia (Cornelia Gillies, was it?), and rarer still when Ormond Eberle asked you a question or replied to one of your own. Miss Gibson never again mentioned your mother: to her, your mother had been a subject, and, once covered, it was closed.

But to you, she was the only subject, the one through which you viewed the world, and therefore it was closed no more than your eyes. In time, of course, your sense of disfellowship ended, but by then only trifles were left to evidence the thirty-three years of her life: a handful of letters, a page or two in a photo album, a few samples of her embroidery, an essay on Portia that had won her a prize, and the prize itself, a book inscribed with her name. But it was her special quality to fade slowly, and while still possessed of her vivid hues, she forever formed your mind, cast it as she might have failed to do alive. And thus, through an odd cycle of affect, perhaps she didn't quite die in 1914. In the way the women of this book have been seen and written of, may she not in some measure have survived?

9 January 1980   JOHN SANFORD

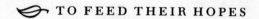 TO FEED THEIR HOPES

Virginia Dare, 1587–(?)

FIRST LADY

BORN: *At Roanoke Island, North Carolina, 18 August 1587, to Eleanor, wife of Ananias Dare, Esq., a daughter, Virginia.*

Nine days later, Governor John White, grandfather of the first English child delivered on American soil, sailed for home for *the present and speedy supply of certain known and apparent lacks and needs, most requisite and necessary.* It took him three years and three hundred and fifty-five days to return, and he found *the houses taken down and the place very strongly enclosed with a high palisade of trees, with curtains and flankers, very fortlike; and one of the chief trees or posts at the right side of the entrance had the bark taken off, and five feet from the ground, in fair capital letters were graven CROTOAN, without any sign or cross of distress.*

He searched for some time, that grandfather of Virginia Dare, but of the one hundred and sixteen souls he had left behind on the dunes, he found no wind-grayed bone, no salt-faded rag, no blurred or bottled word, no word at all save the word *CROTOAN;* he found no stiff scalp with stiffened hair, no coshed-in skull, no scaled pot, no rotten pone, no written word save the word *CROTOAN;* he found no telltale ash, no mildewed trash or unstrung beads, no wax tears from some sprung-for candle, no hound on a grave, no grave on stilts, nothing but the lone and graven word *CROTOAN.*

There were voices on the sand and in the air, but they spoke no tongue that White could understand. There were clouds of heron crying *as if an army of men had shouted together;* there were parrots, falcons, and merlinbaws; there were clam-birds, there were wrens in the cattail, there were plover and willet and clapper-rail—but their cries made no sense in English ears, and the search, begun at that righthand gatepost, ended there. Gazing at the still strange word, White spelled it once aloud, as if charging it to make its own meaning known, but *CROTOAN* it was and only *CROTOAN*, and he reboarded ship and sailed away forever.

Had he stayed longer, would he have found the fact of the matter? Would he have found, in some Indian town, one hundred and sixteen mummied heads on poles? Would he have found their teeth slung on Indian necks, their skin drawn tight on drums? Would he have found the pots in use, the rusted wrecks of tools, the torn Bibles, the clothes again but wrongly worn. . . ?

> DIED: *On or near Roanoke Island, North Carolina, Virginia Dare, daughter of Ananias and Eleanor Dare, on an unknown day between 1587 and 1591.*

Pokahontas, 1595(?)–1617

LADY REBEKAH

It came to pass that in the fifteenth year of her age, Pokahontas, the well-loved daughter of the werowance Powhatan, was promised to a certain lesser chieftain known as Kocoum or, as some heard it said, Cocowam, but that one, however went his name, did not in the end enjoy the felicity of getting the maid to wife.

> *. . . The women are tall and comely made, and they do walk straight and with no common grace. They are very strong of body, full of agility and hardihood, and so inured to extreme that they may couch unsheltered in the rime and rain of winter. . . .*

Pokahontas was lost to her Indian in this fashion. Soon before the ceremonies, she was seen in the company of the Potomacks by the young captain Samuel Argall, and so para-

4

dised was he by her lineaments that he connived at her abduction. With the bribe of a copper kettle, he obtained possession of her person, and, confining her on board of his ship, he removed her to James Towne.

> . . . For raiment, since the women seem not to weave, they use the skins of wild beasts, or, failing these, they make resort to grasses and leaves. But ever are they clad about their middles, for they are shamefast to be seen bare. . . .

There dwelt in that settlement an English gentleman, John Rolfe by name, that lately had come away to the Colonies with his wife. The latter had borne him at Bermuda a girl-child (which was so appelled in honor of the place), but it betided that the woman died upon reaching Virginia. It was after the said calamity that Master Rolfe took his first sight of Pokahontas, and at once he knew for her an ardent desire.

> . . . Some here have their breasts artfully wrought with sundry patterns painted under the flesh. . . .

A desire that was coupled, however, with a higher intention, for Rolfe purposed to wed her. Argall's mind in the matter is unrevealed, but he parted with his prize for the asking, it seems, or at best for a copper kettle. Owning the maid, if maid she still was, Rolfe conceived it his duty at this juncture to imbue her with a soul and thus save her from Satan.

> . . . For all that they are so easily delivered of child, they do cherish their young most dearly. . . .

She requiting his passion, Pokahontas readily gave her consent to being baptized a Christian and named Rebekah, whereupon there was much rejoicing, as ever there is for a brand snatched from the burning, and no great while ensued before plans for espousal were laid.

> . . . A maid may be known from a married woman in this: the maid will shave the fore part of the head close and plait the rest; the other, cutting no part, will plait all. . . .

5

The marriage was solemnized in the church at James Towne. A goodly number of the Colony were present at the peculiar but proper union, as were a deputation of Algonkwin savages from Werowocomoco. These last in general comported themselves well, though some were seen to relieve their stresses, as children do, in that place where they sat or stood.

> . . . For a visitor of note, the naturals provide a woman as bedfellow, she first being reddened with the powder of a dried root that they call pocone. . . .

From England now, advices to Master Rolfe acquaint him that various enterprises were in need of his vigilance, from which it followed that he took passage in a ship early departing the settlement. With him went his wife Rebekah, and after the perils of voyaging, they made safe arrival oversea. There Master Rolfe shewed his strange companion to the Court, which most graciously did receive her, and then how the people did run in her train through the halls and streets of London!

> . . . The women, though burdened with all manner of drudgery, the while their men pleasure in wars and hunting, yet do they bear their years well. . . .

In that city was domiciled Captain John Smith, the same that Pokahontas once had saved the beating out of his brains by her father's braves, and that ever since she had so scarce seen as to suppose him no longer living. He, learning of her proximity, came now into her presence, making a leg, as to royalty, and calling her Lady Rebekah.

> . . . These women in their troths will seek a great distance of blood from that of their husbands, close consanguinity being repugnant to custom. . . .

Thus addressed by him, she turned away her face, it may be for hurt at no warmer welcome from one so cherished that she had claimed his life. And thereafter a sickness became seated in her, and she wasted sorely till in the *George*, the ship that was to take her back to Virginia, she died. None had told her, for none knew or remembered, that in Hebrew, whence the name, the meaning of Rebekah was *the noose*.

> . . . *A chief ruler or king of those people has as many women as he will for his needs.* . . .

Bereft by this latest frown of fortune, Master Rolfe went himself in the *George* to James Towne, and there he met and wedded with the woman Jane Peirce. He did not live out five more years. The naturals killed him in a massacre.

Anne Hutchinson, 1590(?)–1643

THOSE TOTAL DEPRAVITIE BLUES

I doe cast you out and deliver you up to Sathan.
—Rev. John Wilson

Anne Hutchinson, being called before the Great and Generall Court of Masachuset and there charged with having comported herself in a sedityous maner, which is to say a maner tending to promoat hatred, stryfe, and discontent, and having sware to the truth of the Testimony she was about to give, did depose and say, not without contumacie, that she denyed the allegation and defyed the allegator.

The learned and reverend Court poynted out that in mayntayning a Covenant of Grace to be superiour to a Covenant of Workes, the accused had flowne in the face of the establisht Creede, whereupon she avouched that the Lord Jesus Christ had revealed Himself to her and ingendered her belief, this to the horrour of the Assemblage, for to Sedityon must now be added the graver charge of Anabaptysme, a cult accurst since John of Leyden's daie.

In despite of the common dismaie, still did the accused persist in her antinomian wordes and waies, saying that the Saviour had not stopt speaking to the world in 22d Revelation. Contrarywise, she said, He was speaking at that very moment, nor was the last worde even yet spoken. Moreover, she saw fitt to add, He dwelt in her Boddie, a bright and morning Starre, and He litt the dark, wherefor she needed not to go with eies upon the ground in shayme of Adam's sinne. Nay, she said, she was saved by the saving grace of Jesus Christ within.

This avowance did produce among the convocation a most violent Appall, as tho the Fiend himself had been heard. When shocke abated, it was observd that what the woman had said was the rankest of Heresys, in that she claymed a mirracle in a time when mirracles were past, thereby setting the Booke at naught. She was not by this dire dictum silenced. Rather did she seeme to become the more frowarde, for she repeated that Christ was insyde her and stirring, infusing her spirrit wondrouslie.

It was now clear to the Court that if these Hereticall teachings were not supprest, the rule of the Cloth was at an end in Masachuset. Should it be suffered that the people believe each of them contayned a moietie of the Holy Ghoast, or conscience, as the woman called it, then all would sitt in judgement of their owne Actes, and being God and man in one, none would condemn himself for sinne and none be damned, not though he be so deprayved as she.

Upon due deliberation, it was found that the woman Hutchinson had become informed by a divelish Dellusion, rendering her unfitt for the society of that place, and the sentence of the Court was that for having troubled the Church with Lyes and Errour, she be declared a Leper and constrayned to withdraw from the Congregation and the Collony.

It remaynes but to discrive her departure and that brieflie. Suffice it that in her pryde, she went with necke unbent, back strait, and steppe firm, abating not a jot her demeanour before the Court. Certain clods and clapperclawes made it their busines to tell her that she had got her comings, and they made shift to spitte upon her garments and in her road, but she scorned them, saying *Better to be cast from the Church than to denye Christ*, and she was gonne.

Shortlie after her excommunication, it was reported to the Clergie and Magistrates of Masachuset that the Exile had been deliverd of a monstrous Birth. This she would fain have lett on to be an hydatidiforme Mole were it not for a Mr. Clarke, physition, who accuratlie defined the material exprest by her Privities. It was a membrayne, he said, stuft with jags and dollops of flesh, twenty-six in number, some contayning winde and some water, and some were hard-composed, like the lobe of a Livver, but all were possest of a most melancholie stinke. There was no secundine, he averred, and this alone would have served to nominate the true father of the ejectamenta—not man, God forfend, but Diabolus!

Mary Dyer, (?)–1660

PASS NOT OVER THE BROOK

In the name of the Lord Jesus Christ, I do declare thee, Anne Hutchinson, to be cast out from this church, a heathen and a publican from this day forth, and I do deliver thee unto Sathan for the destruction of thy flesh.
—Rev. John Wilson

As Anne, damned, went toward the door, there was one that rose and went with her and took her by the hand. Her name was Mary Dyer, and against her too now time began to run.

They say of her that she was a person of no mean extract, of piercing knowledge in many things, grave and comely and wondrous fit for great affairs, but they say this as well, that she contained a proud spirit and was much addicted to revelations. She held the Gospel to be evergreen and growing, a never-blowing bloom, a tale always in the telling, now and on the morrow as once in Palestine. The Book signified nothing to her: if it embraced the Word, it was the Word lifeless, movable type that moved no more. The living Word was the Light within, and each man glowed with it, lit his own way—each was a lamp from which Jesus shone out on the world.

Odd to the mind of the ministry, some few of her kind were even odder to the eye. There were those who went about with pans of burning brimstone on their heads, and others blacked their faces or, in token of an empty sermon, broke an empty bottle in the pews, and two zealous goodies publicized their privates in the road. But the durable sin of the Ranters was their ranting, which to many of the people was something more than senseless sound: a sweet belief, they found it, that each should be father, each son, each the paraclete.

A sweet belief, but it got them bark in the pulpit and bite in the street, it got them spittle and avoidance, and when, as often, the pure felt the itch, they were frisked for a hellish signature, the triple tits of a witch. It got them knotted cords on the bare back, fines and close confinement, a hot spike through the tongue, and an amulet to wear, a pair of their ears. Their Inner Light got them outer darkness—exile—and the penalty for coming home, for crossing the vales below the Mount of Olives. . . .

On the day that thou passeth over the brook Kidron, thou shalt surely die.

And yet four crossed over and were cast in jail, and Mary, ravished by the love of the living God within her, followed in their trail. She lay there long with them, and then she was freed and sent away. But stay she could not, and upon her second return, she was tried and given death, and they stood her on the gallows, tied her skirts, covered her face with Mr. Wilson's kerchief—and reprieved her!

She still lived, but she would not accept her life from those that persecuted her. Expelled once more, she once more came back, and this time they kicked the ladder out from under her feet, and on the forbidden side of the brook, she was dead.

10

Katharine Tekakwitha, 1656–80

KATHARINE, BRIDE OF CHRIST

Jesus, I love Thee!
—last words

Lily of the Mohawks, they called her. She was born in Ossernenon, which is a village at no great distance from Fort Orange, or Albany, as now the place is known. Her mother, a baptized Algonquin, and her father, a pagan Chief of the Agniers tribe, were both of them swept away by the smallpox when the child was scarcely four years old. She herself, *la pauvre petite*, did not escape unscathed, suffering vesiculations that left her with a pitted skin, and with sight so impaired that ever after she could not bear the light of the sun and had to wear a veil. *First Virgin of the Iroquois*, she was called, and this too, for she was saintly, *the New World Geneviève*.

She was eleven before she saw her first missionary, and one would have thought her long lost by then in the error of savage ways, and yet, *Deo favente*, it was not so. Early in youth, the qualities of her soul became known to all, and even in her pagan state, she was, it is not too much to say, already a Christian. There was about her a sweet and seemly meekness of spirit, a modesty altogether foreign to her kind, a virtue white and blinding, this too in contrast with the habits and traditions of her people. That love of virginity—how shall it be accounted for save by a special grace of the Holy Ghost!

Of this maid, sprung from some Heaven-sent seed, her own savage people said, *She knows but two houses, her own and the church*, and they spoke truly: the Passion was part of her from the start of her life, and she strove through its brief course to endure it in her flesh, even as the Lamb had done. Once each week, she performed the Sacrament of Penance, with her a most severe austerity, for she observed it by scourging herself with thorny switches, or engaging another

11

to deal her the strokes. And she was much given to fasting, or, when she partook of food, to mixing it with ash, all this in denial of the things of this life. And there was more, for she wore a girdle studded with sharpened points of iron, and she scorched her feet like a slave's to signify her slavery to Christ, and there were occasions when she tried her faith by fire, placing live coals betwixt her toes for as long as an *Ave Maria* would require, and she strewed her pallet with burr and brier, that she might enjoy no night of rest, and, in final mortification, she swore she would be a virgin till she died, all this for Him on the Cross. She became His Bride at twenty-four, expiring in a quiet and gentle agony, an end so peaceful that those who were there were for a while unaware that she had gone.

Wonders followed apace. Hardly had the maid ceased to be than her scars and the mutilations of illness ceased as well: her wasted body bloomed even as priest and savage watched, and her face, pocked and sored and slashed, grew to be beautiful, beautiful! and it soon began to smile. And this wonder too was told, of an appearance she had made in the hour of her death to a woman who had prayed, and this, that at her obsequies on the ensuing day, a priest trying to intone the *Vexilla* could not pass the first two words for the sudden weeping that was heard in the church, strange cries of grief that came to fill the air. And these things began to be said, that earth from her grave had wrought cures of fevers, congestions of the chest, diseases of the foot and hip, and there were those who reported that the deaf were made to hear and the dumb were given speech, and her crucifix too had worked miraculous recoveries, and her garments, and a plate from which she had eaten—indeed, whatever she had touched, wherever she had passed, there great radiance was, there proof of the power of Heaven, and her people revered her.

Holy Father, Sovereign Pontiff, they wrote, *this is our reason for writing to you. We shall exult with great joy if you will agree that we may venerate and invoke her in our church in the same way that other Saints are invoked. If you will*

12

*kindly favor us, it will make our hearts happy, our conduct
good, and our children will grow up perfect and realize the
glory of Heaven.*

Virgin Bride of the Lord

THE UNDERGROUND STREAM

*Then said Mary unto the angel, How shall this be, seeing
I know not a man?*
—Luke 1:34

She knew no man, nor did man know her, know when
she was born, how long she lived on earth, or how or whether
she died. None can say with certainty that she was a Nazarene
from the hills of Galilee, but some do say it, and no less sure
are they that put her place of birth at Jerusalem, aye, and
near to the Pool of Probatica, but verily neither camp knows,
for she knew no man, nor was she known. Mother of God,
deiparous Mary, not even her lineage is clear: her father may
have been Joachim, a sheepman rich in flocks, and her
mother the prophetess Anna (James the Less tells of these
things), and right it is that their names when taken together
spell *Grace prepared by God*, the which might well foretoken
a Mary of David's royal race. Yet save that faith alone is truth,
we know little more than this, that she came, brought the
Light of the World, bore it in her unwanton womb, and later
went away.

The river Mary, out of darkness bearing light, why must
she have glistened first in Palestine, why may she not have
risen radiant here? Why must it be supposed she surfaced in
or above the vale of Esdraelon or close to where one day her
christine Son would die? Why up from gneiss or schist or por-
phyry must she have come, why from some limestone fault
must she have shone, some millet meadow of Nazareth, some
mount whereon grew olives? Why could she not have brought

13

her sunglow here, begun, the Virgin, with this virgin forest? Why, where no names were on the land or waters, could she not have dawned, flooded the wilderness with day? Mary, river of light, why could she not have lit this undiscovered, this kingless kingdom—this still immaculate *here*?

Mrs. Prudence Whitwell, 1740–73

USED ONLY ONCE

PRUDENCE the Wife of the Revd WILLIAM WHITWELL, departed this Life Feb^ry the 7th 1773. AE 33

It was as good as new, the stone he bought her, and few would know or care that its face had been wrought before. There was that lower case *r* afloat between the lines of letters, and there were traces of erasures, the ghosts of former words, and pits of old punctuation now accentuated space—but Time, the Rev^d may've thought, would wear such things away.

It'd worn her, Time had (it or niggard Whitwell), borne her to the grave at the age of thirty-three. Time's sand had ground her down, or was her hone the whetstone Whitwell? Prudence would know, and so would her bone and ash: having read the Rev^d living, she could recite the Rev^d dead. Aye, Prudence could tell of Whitwell much, his fist of a soul and his penny-wisdom, and she alone can say if this is true, that before she was buried, he removed her shoes, used, of course, but as good as new.

Phillis Lyndon, 1746(?)–73

BURYING-GROUND ON FAREWELL STREET

She was free from the common vices.
—Rev. Ezra Stiles, Newport, R.I.

A nigger-servant to the Governor is what she was and got from Guinea, got when half her life was over (at thirteen!), and, married to another nigger-servant, Brother Zingo, she bore a few more servants, and then her second half was done, and she was dead, she was a dead nigger. But, as the Rev. Ezra said, *she was free from the common vices and walked soberly*, and, nigger or not, she'd earned a place for her body to lie while her soul ascended from Rhode Island, wherefore he let her be buried in a far corner of his churchyard, and when the wind was right, it was hard to tell she was there.

In time, the wind brought with it nothing but the salted savor of the Bay, and *nigger* came to be forgotten when the nigger's name was read. *In memory of Phillis*, it says on her tomb, and winged Phillis, shown between the crossed Darts of Death, gazes (at whom?), gazes white-featured from the stone. What betrays her is that child she holds, what gives her away is that flat nose and those black slate curls of hair.

Sarah Johnson, 1766–90

HER SOUL A VERY SUN

Whose Rays out Shine all pimping Stars
—Edward Taylor

Read, in her red sandstone, of the virtues she took to the grave. *This lovely Fair* was one year wed when buried here, dead merely in the flesh, in the Good Deed deathless. Read, within this florid frame, of her chaste behavior, her manner

mild, her piety, read of this dear, this cheerful partner gone
so soon from her partner's bed and bedded under a chase of
scrolls and gourds, under pimping stars and a staring winged
face. Read of seraphic chemicals that nourish only weed.

Ann Putnam and Abigail Williams, 1692

TWO OF SALEM'S AFFLICTED CHILDREN

Thou shalt not suffer a witch to live.
—Exodus 22:18

Ah, but they were sore beset, that pair, poor Ann, pure
Abigail, it was more than flesh could bear, the fits and keck-
ing, the bitten wrists, the pin-pricks, the sudden levitations—
whish! whish! whish!, they'd cry, and then they'd be made to
fly through the air, they said, though no visible force was
wielded, for no one else was there. They suffered seizures of
the bowels, they said, as if their puddings were coming out,
and voices spoke to them in skimble-skamble, and they swore
to ghostly apparitions, among these a black man offering a
journey to a golden city, and there were yellow birds, they
claimed—*Look where Goodwife C. sits suckling her yellow
bird!*—and they saw a sacrament of witches where red drink
was taken and red bread eaten that was compounded of rye
meal and children's void. Small wonder, then, that their tor-
mentors were found and tried and sent to hell—nineteen
woman warlocks went, and Giles Corey, pressed to death,
pointed out the way. *Thou shalt not suffer a witch to live,* so
spake the Lord, and twenty so deemed were damned, twenty
died of the Williams child, twenty died of Ann.

There were no more hangings, no more punishments
forte et dure, and Salem was as before, walking with God
uprightly in the light of day, whitely walking in the ways of
the Lord, and it knew not now the vexing of other days: Satan
and his imps were gone. But Ann was there, and Abigail, and

a time was coming when they'd bite themselves again, and they'd bring a book to be signed, and a number of yellow birds.

Pearl Prynne, in *The Scarlet Letter*

AD LIBS BY A FICTITIOUS CHARACTER

Child, what art thou?
Oh, I am your little Pearl!
—Nathaniel Hawthorne

As Mr. Hawthorne says, the first thing I saw was the scarlet *A* on the breast of my mother's gown. It was a nearby brightness in a gray-green world, and it drew me as any other would've done, a red flower, a red bird or berry, or fire as it played. It was there at the start, and it stayed, as much a part of Hester as her eyes. But Mr. Hawthorne seems to have been unaware of the second thing I saw, a strange lack since it was a second *A*, this one black.

I was three months old at the time and in my mother's arms on the pillory, pilloried too, the fruit of her sin and therefore no less vile than she. All Boston had come to view us, and faces paved the market place, paned the windows, grew on trees. There was an absence of color in the crowd—the uniform garb was black—but a certain conical hat seemed somehow blacker than the rest, and so too a certain cape that fell in folds and flared, and I stared at the shape my father thus made: a sable *A* on a sable field.

I seemed to know him at sight, though I've never known how. He stood among the crowd, concealed by it, as he thought, like a shadow lost in the shadow night, but there was my begetter, the black letter *A*. Dimmesdale! Mr. Hawthorne says I touched him once (it was at the Governor's, he claims, and I was going on three), but if so, I must've done it to test whether one who looked so dead was still alive. His eyes were

17

deep in his head, bits of sky in a well, and his hair lay sense-less, nonconductive, and his skin was dry, like slough. If, as said, I touched him once, let it be known that once was all, but quite enough.

My mother must've touched him too, and not his hand, as I did, nor merely with her cheek; it must've been some other member that she reached, sunless, sallow. Mr. Haw-thorne describes the result of that collision—I, a wild and flighty elf named Pearl, an airy child, the friend of weeds, sticks, rags, and the *ferae* found in the forest. He dwells long, Mr. Hawthorne, on the wrong they worked on me, but mum's the word on why. How could she have borne him bare, how endured that prying candle, that tallow finger in her private hair? and where, in what field did she lie, what pinebough bed, to what rocks was her fall revealed? and did she cry aloud when his small flame singed her, did she pray when he came or wait till he went? Ah, the reverend Arthur! Pale psalmer, scratcher of itches, charmer of skirts, snake in the pubic grass—what did she find in his leached-out phiz, what soul sat behind those rank clothes, what imbued his sour stuffing?

To my mind, she sinned only in sinning with him. It was her affair that she chose to be ridden, and I didn't care where the rider took her, on the run or standing still or during a swim in a stream—but to receive such a one and make him my father! to couple with that quick-spent dip, that one-cent wick! my God, to be lit but once and then so dimly! And thereafter, for seven years, she wore the badge where the world could see it, while he sequestered his in his room. It was not enough that he carved it with a whip, it didn't matter that it bled and festered and appeared to glow in the dark: he let my mother alone be stoned by eyes.

Mr. Hawthorne says that she took me overseas when he died and, after a span of years, returned without me, and rumor ran that writings reached her from time to time, some wearing seals of an unknown bearing, and that monies made her late days easy and paid for the slate over her bones and Arthur's. But with no blood of my own, is it likely that blood would wed me? With no name but Pearl, would I be apt to

18

flash his ring and bring to bed some belted earl, would I become My Lady, would I be called My Lady Pearl? Or would I, so to say, lie below nobility and sell what Hester had given away?

Eunice Williams, 1696–1786

A PRISONER OF THE INDIANS

I could not prevaile with her to go home. After long Solicitations, may be not, *a plaine denyall, were all we could gett from her in allmost two hours time.*
—Col. John Schuyler, 1713

She was seven years old when the Caughnawagas and the French fell on Deerfield. Attacking in the last hours of a winter's night, they took the settlement by surprise, and they were past the coldcocked sentries and inside the palisade before colonial eyes were fairly open to realize the foe in the dark. By then, there was blood everywhere, the snow was slashed with red wine, and there were forty-nine dead and dying in beds and doorways and lying in the drifts, wherefore barely had the day begun when for many a one it ended. One hundred and eleven captives were taken, and for most of these the end came on other days along the hard way to Quebec: the white world killed them, and hunger cost them no few lives, and they died too of hope lost as the miles grew. Eunice outlived the march by eighty-three years.

For sundry whites, the Indians accepted ransom, and these went back to what was left of Deerfield, but for Eunice, no. There must've been some quality in the child that made them swear they'd part with their hearts before they let her go, there must've been some singularity they saw in the little pale sister—or did they merely see themselves? Well it may be, and like enough she saw herself in them, and when Schuyler tried to beguile her home, she replied *Zaghte oghte,* which is to say, *May be not,* a plain denial.

19

In Deerfield, they never understood, those who'd survived the raid. They thought she'd been denatured by Jesuitical teachings, vaticanized and led into popish ways; they thought, her mind amaze, she'd strayed to the Scarlet Woman. They laid her fall to the black-robed priests—it was they, the black-robed dimmesdales thought, who'd lured their lamb away. There among the ruins and graves of Deerfield, none would ever hold that she'd been driven, not drawn, from the fold: she was only seven, poor thing, when seduced from Heaven.

After a great many years, she came back a time or two, but only for a visit, nor did she tarry long. She was priest-married by then to an Indian, one Amrusus, an Algonquin, or it might've been Ambrusus, a corruption of the French Ambroise, and by him she'd borne three children (four, some say), all of them baptized. But the children, of course—like the union, indeed, like the father's name—were attainted by the Whore beyond the mountain, damned in the Church of Rome.

Martha Washington, 1731(?)–1802

WHEN I CAST MY EYES TOWARD BELVOIR

. . . memento of former pleasures. . . .
—George Washington to Sally Fairfax

Five-and-twenty years, he wrote, had nearly passed away, and still (and his wife knew it), still his eyes would stray and yearn downstream to burned Belvoir, miles of stream to piles of ash, still, so late in the day, would he turn to where the fire of old had been. How often in those years she must've seen him gaze away at distance, sometimes in the dark, how hard to bear, his smile for someone else though no one else was there, his absences while present, his thoughts of other rooms, other junctions, how hard for her to bear, his twenty-five years upstream from a dream that was not yet ended!

20

And so to Sally so long in England, he wrote of happy moments spent in her company, *the happiest of my life*, he said, and his wife, being shown the letter, merely read what she'd always known. She may have wondered what she might've done to break the spell, what dress she might've worn, what airs, wondered what books she might've read, what wisdom uttered, wondered, even, what winning ways she might've used in bed. But watching him watch through the window (for what? what would rise from Belvoir's ruins?) she knew that the spell once cast would last till he died. That was then but a year away, very near forever.

Mrs. Benedict Arnold, 1760–1804

AFTER GREAT SUFFERING

. . . he expired without a groan.
—Peggy Shippen Arnold

He died on the 14th of June, 1801—*at ½ past six in the morning*, she wrote—died of a dropsy and the gout and some affliction of the throat. In the *Gentleman's Magazine*, there was a note about the occurrence, and mention was made of the seven mourning coaches and four state carriages that formed the funeral cavalcade from Gloucester Place to Battersea. The widow rode in the first vehicle, directly behind the hearse taking her Brigadier toward the Thames and, beyond the river, a grave in the yard of St. Mary's Church.

It was a long hard road that he'd come, but *Gentleman's* had nothing to say of its many turns and many crossings, its acclivities and descents, or the way it had dwindled at times to no road at all. Three lines told of the General's latter end, but no fourth dwelt on how he'd come there. To *Gentleman's*, perhaps it didn't matter that a traitor had fled his own his native rope to die (without a groan) a foreign body in an outland bed. To his bereaved in weeds, it mattered much.

When this ride through London was over, she'd still be alive, still be passing quality in the Row or on the Ring or as she crossed a square. She'd still have to bear the silent staring, the smiles with cold teeth, the eyes that seemed off-center, as if trained on something behind her, or, worse, those that were quite undetained and simply slid away. She heard hoofs and harness, wheels, the leathers bracing the springs, she saw faces through the windows, leaves, sky, a flag on the fly from a spire. Like the one aspread on the casket, she may have thought, and she could almost feel it, properly folded, weighing on her hands when the coffin was out of sight.

It'd be more toilsome now to play the lamb, to sham surprise, to let on that she hadn't known of letters in code, traffic with spies, the sale of sterling honor for sterling silver. It'd be more galling, the hope she'd had for a title—Lady Arnold, they'd be calling her if André hadn't been caught, and the corpse ahead would've been Lord. Why did he have to die when he did, how could he have done this to her, left her to wear his guilt while she tried to hide her own? The cortège halted for a moment—some crosscurrent at a green corner—and then it moved on again between two rows of trees.

Why had she ever married him?, she may have wondered. So much older than she, crippled, crabbed, always sensing a slight, a spleeny sort, he was, sour and flaring, overweening, and in the end, he'd chaffered for his price. André—ah, there was quite a different sort, and to her dying day, she thought, she'd keep his lock of hair. That day was three years hence, and when she died of cancer of the womb, they'd put the manquée lady beside her manqué lord. *Gentleman's* would carry no word of the event.

Sally Hemings, 1773–1835

BLACK SALLY

Of all the damsels on the green,
On mountain, or in valley,
A lass so luscious ne'er was seen
As Monticellian Sally. . . .
                    —anti-Jefferson crambo

Only a quarter of her blood was black, and it gave her
the merest tinge, a skin just barely darker dinged than a
Saxon's would've been: white, it seemed, when seen in certain light. Her mother was a mulatto, and her grandmother
was black all the way back to the sixth day of creation, further,
even, if her Maker was a buck—but Sally?: her face was the
color of coral in cream. A beauty, all who saw her say, well-
made, well-mannered, and, but for that tar, that far-off taint,
a lady. Instead, she was a slave, and Jefferson owned her, and
she knew his bed, or bedside, for eight-and-thirty years: it
would've been longer, but he died.

She could read and write, and she conversed in French,
at times no doubt with him, and it was his delight to dress her
prettily and beribbon her hair, which was fine, full, undulant,
and, yes, quite black, on her mons too, more than likely.
He'd've known for certain; he got seven children in that tan-
talizing maze. A most comely queen, his quadroon must've
been, to engage so much of such a one so long.

In his private writings, her name appears seldom, and
then as Sally only and always as a slave, as if he'd withheld
their true relation even from his pen. Or did someone censor
the letters he left, the farm and garden books, the anas, the
journals, did someone try to whiten him for the ages, cleanse
his pages of the tincture black? But it was only the word that
was omitted or expunged: the flesh was there all the time, a
bisque presence that many knew and more were aware of.
Within those palladian walls, she was everywhere just short
of forty years, free, the captivating slave, to roam the halls, to

go from room to room, and in one of those, where she and the master slept, she owned the master.

What was said through all those nights, what thoughts did she have and what thoughts he, under that ceiling of his, under him, what did she derive but seed, and in her high-yellow upheavals, what did she give, did she dwell on freedom, did he make those seven children and never hear? Well, she was still there, or near, down to the day he died.

Susan and Betsy Roberts, c. 1775–(?)

SISTERS ON THE NATCHEZ TRACE

Their names are known and not much more than the color of their hair, and as to that, few can say now which was the blonde, which the brunette. No likenesses remain, nothing in charcoal, nil in silhouette, no spoken word was ever taken down, and they seem to drift through history mute as smoke, and soon, like smoke, they disappear—but not before they give some of their savor to the air, the woods, the winding way of the wilderness road.

With Micajah and Wiley—Big Harpe and Little Harpe—they came west from Carolina through the Cumberland Gap. It was never clear who was wedded to whom, for both men bedded both women, and always Susan's belly billowed, always Betsy's womb was full. They went hatless, all four, and they dressed in leather, deerskin, one would suppose, or was it the hide of those who'd died, were slain, along the road? They were there, the women, when the Harpes lay wait at fords and defiles for come what may—they were among the rocks, they were close by in the canebrake, when the peddlers were shot or clubbed, the wayfarers, the rash and cash-laden, the lone yeoman going home, they watched the stripping of the bodies, the gutting, the burials in streams. In the family way or giving the tit, or nursing and big-bellied both, there they were, the women, passing the time of day or spatting over stolen shoes.

The Harpes wound up with their heads cut off and propped in the crotch of a tulip tree. The women lived on, it's said, found worthy men, led virtuous lives, sent forth sons to sire other Harpes, daughters to suckle other sisters, and when their hour came, Susan and Betsy doubtless died.

Charlotte Temple, in *Charlotte Temple* (1791)

A TALE OF TRUTH

But, ah! the cruel spoiler came—
—Susanna Rowson (1761–1824)

Among her pages, fact and figment wind, a wreathe of myth and actual, and you wonder whether Charlotte lived or floated through her mind, and the spoiler, you wonder, did he breathe once and wither what breathing touched, or was he merely something written, someone to be read. But no matter—he came, you're told in the story, when scarcely fifteen summers had shone on Charlotte's head, and before another knew her, the strayed one was dead, a shade in the yard of Trinity. Her stone has fallen on its back, and grass has overgrown it, vagued it at the edges, and it seems to lie displayed on plush. It wears no date or boss, only the good name lost to Montraville. (or Montresor, as he was known in life, forty years of age, wed and well so, with ten children and a wife, a Royal Artificer, the word in his trade for Engineer)—Montraville or Montresor, one knave or the other, or both if the same, put Charlotte to shame and laid her in the grave. And then away and home to England sailed Montraville the fiction or Montresor the real, and with him went his fistula and his dreadful hydrocele—ill now, the cruel spoiler, and in the cruel hands of the Sisters Three.

Well, there's the tale, true or otherwise, the article or a

dream adrift in a dream. But it's all one to Charlotte, a long while lying below the pointed pile of Trinity, a bearing once for ships and birds, a pharos they saw from the sea. It's hidden now, the spire, sunk in the risen city, and the ships and birds steer by higher things. Only at meridian does the sun find the deep-down steeple and the ground around its feet; only then do the headstones warm and the dead arise, and Fulton's soul joins Gallatin's, and Hamilton's and Charlotte's stroll.

Nancy Ward, c. 1738–1822

A WHITE INDIAN

Beloved children of the Cherokee nation, your mothers beg of you not to part with any more of our land. . . .
— Nancy, at the age of seventy-nine
to the last Council of Chiefs, 1817

She was too old by then, too sick to attend in person, wherefore she had to send in her stead an extension of herself, a thing whose mere presence would summon up her name, and what she chose for the agency was her lame-stick, a cane so singularly wrought that all who saw it saw too Tame Doe's daughter. It rested there among the Chiefs, part of the seated circle and partaking of the fire, and through it they addressed her, and few it failed to speak to in reply. The cane was hers, hence it was she, *Nanye'hi,* or, as the whites miscalled her, Nancy.

Your mothers beg of you, she said, the Beloved Woman to her beloved Cherokees, but it was much too late for such pleas as she made that day. They'd been Indians once, wild and without pity, iroquoian, and time was when they'd slain in all directions, killed the British for the French, and, the other way 'round, the French for the British, and killed for both their brother Creeks. On each of those occasions, it'd been she, Tame Doe's daughter, who'd brewed their tea of holly leaves, the Black Drink a brave would down to stave off

26

death in war. And it'd been she, though none knew why, who'd warned the whites of their coming, sent her white lover on ahead to give away their numbers and the route they'd take to Watauga, she who'd turned white defeat to red, and done the dark deed twice.

And now, late, late, she was begging them to hold, to fight the whites some more. How could they have fought, and if they could've done so, how could they have won? They were only the remains of a nation, they were potters, weavers, taverners, they were a people that rode in wagons now and were drugged by the smell of soap. How could such have stemmed the whites, that were running west like dawn, how could they have killed the light of day? She'd cost them too much, their *Nanye'hi*—Tennessee was lost.

Some, sitting there, may have wondered why she'd betrayed them, and some, staring at the fire, may have wondered why they'd let her live, and some, smoking, may have wondered when she'd die. But no one spoke his mind—who could've fathomed such things?—and the Chiefs, if they still were men, were content to sit like shades, to smoke, to speak across the fire, to dream of bygone days, to seem. . . .

Nanye'hi had five more years to live, and when the time came for the spirit to leave her, a brightness would be seen to rise from her body, and it would glide around the room, a glowing bird, and then fly away toward Chote, the Cherokee city of refuge, where the evil were forever safe, cowards, liars, thieves, murderers, even white Indians.

Nancy Hanks Lincoln, 1784(?)–1818

A RESTING PLACE IN INDIANA

They say she died of the milksick at the age of thirty-four, and they say, those who may have buried her, that her grave is near a deer run along a branch of Pigeon Creek. Word of mouth, all of it; no one really knows. Death being an everyday thing—it came, did its work, and went—and hers being the same small event, it drew small mention if it later crossed the mind: *Tom lost his woman last fall*, a neighbor may have said, *or was it the last but one?* No more than that, though, for the plague carried off too many to remember, and in time it was hard to name the dead, the order of their going, and those they'd left behind. And so there was little about this particular occasion, in truth almost nothing, to set it apart from the rest: Tom's woman, if Tom's she was, was borne toward Pigeon Creek and there put away in the earth, and at night the deer, precise and tentative, highstep overhead.

She'd come far for that burying, from a place called Mikes Run, it was said, or from Keyser, wherever that was, or from Bare Bones on the Namozine road, or, as some averred, from Little Falling River in Virginia. But no one knew at the time, and no one knows yet, nor has it been learned how to spell her name—*Hanks*, was it, or *Hankes* with an *e*, or *Hawkes*, or was she a natural child with no family name at all? There were no auguries of coming, no halcyon birds were seen, no glowing appeared in the sky, and with scarcely a trace of her presence, a picture to prove her being, a letter or signature, initials on a tree or wall, she'd seem to have been a fancy, someone's dreamery. Still, there's that grave down under the deer run, and whoever lies there hears them come at night to graze and drink till wolves are blazoned by the wind. Why may it not be she?

Sacajawea, 1788(?)–1884(?)

CHARBONNEAU'S WOMAN

Frenchman's squaw came to our camp who belongs to the Snake nation.
—John Ordway's journal, 1804

She was sixteen or so when she turned up at Fort Mandan, and she was owned by a *voyageur*, his wife, possibly, or she might've been something he'd won at dice, taken in trade, found in the wild rice or the reeds. But however he'd gotten her, she was great in the belly when she dogged him to the gate and squatted down outside while he went in and tried for work. *A Mr Chaubonie Came to See us*, wrote Captain Clark. *This man wished to hire as an interpiter*. According to the trappers of the region, he was a sneak and a knave, and the Indians gave him spiteful titles—"Chief of the Little Village," they called him, and "Great Horse from Afar." All the same, though he spoke in tokens, he was taken on: his Snake squaw could speak Shoshone.

No two agreed on the spelling of her name, but there was no spelling, really, merely syllables of sound—Sa-ca-ja-we-a—that rarely twice running were written the same. But what did it matter—Sa-ka-ka-we-a, Sah-kar-gar-we-a, Tsi-ki-ka-wi-as? She was only an Indian, slight, small, quiet, shy of whites—what did it matter, and what did she? Still, to Clark, to Lewis, she seemed well worth waiting for, and wait they did till her child was born. Jean Baptiste, he was christened (in Shoshone, he was known as Pomp), and borne in a scabbard on his mother's back, he set out for the Pacific with the expedition.

The next time he saw Fort Mandan, he was eighteen months old, and he was ending a round trip of five thousand miles: he'd peered at half a country before it sported names, the Yellowstone, Lemhi Pass, the Bitterroot Range. From his perch, he'd seen his mother reading sign—moccasin prints, peeled pine trees, telltale stones; seen her find food the whites would've missed, serviceberries and purple currants, roots, camas, yampa, all these good to eat; seen her weave, launder, dress meat—aye, and dress wounds. And through it all, the cold, the rains, the hunger, the hostiles, she'd never been heard to whine or clamor, as the Canuck did, for she laid claim to nothing; indeed, she'd parted with much, her blue-bead belt, which she prized, to buy a robe for Clark, and once she'd given him even more, a piece of bread she'd saved for little Pomp.

Some say she died young, of a putrid fever at twenty-five, and some say she was still alive at an ancient age, but there are no proofs among the Indians, only stories told and heard and once more told, the ever-inconstant word. No one therefore knows whether it's she who lies under that rock on the Wind River Reservation, having lived, it seems, till yesterday. Well may she have died far from there, down where the Knife flows into the Missouri, and far away too in time.

Ann Rutledge, 1813–35

THE SILVER FIGMENT

I shall assuredly remain firm in my conviction that
Ann Rutledge, is a myth.
—Mary Todd Lincoln

I am Ann, they say her tombstone reads, *Ann, who sleeps beneath these weeds,* and they say her lover lay by the grave all night, embraced the rounded earth, the mound of fill, till people came and led the man away, and they say, those who thought they knew, that he never loved again, never Mary—how could he?, when he'd died himself, there beside dead Ann. A myth, his wife called it, a manufacture of the mind, the coin of Billy Herndon, sottish, unkind, odious Billy, and so it may have been, a coinage, all of it, minted in envy, uttered in revenge, so it may have been. It wears well, though, as it goes from hand to hand, aye, it even grows.

Mrs. Edgar Allan Poe, 1821–47

A DOLL THAT BLED

Love shall heal my weakened lungs.
—Virginia Poe

She was wearing a white dress when it happened. She was fingering a harp and singing through its strings, and all at

once she seemed to grow a scarf of blood that kept on growing, grew into a para red pinafore, spread, fringing and rav-
eling, until it reached the floor. And five years later, in an
acrostic valentine, she'd say to him *Love shall heal my weakened lungs*, but she'd be nearly dead then, and only death
would stop the bleeding.

The white dress—what became of it? Was it stained beyond saving, was it torn when taken off, was it draped across
a chair, dropped, flung toward some corner, was it hung up to
dry, or was she allowed to lie as she was, asprawl in reddened
rags? It's said that children loved to play with her, wherefore
the dress must've been pretty once, edged with lace and rib-
boned, and there must've been a pink smile on the face, and
the hair, the eyes, the shoes, they were black, were they
not?, and shone. They loved to pet her, it's said, hold her
hand, feed her candy, play at being grown. They loved to play
with her, children did, and she with them.

Maria Clemm, 1790–1871

MOTHER OF VIRGINIA, MOTHER-IN-LAW
OF POE

I want $5 or even three, *cannot you procure it for me
somehow, oh if you could only know how much I am in
need of it.*
                          —"Muddie" (Maria Clemm)

She was still begging in 1865. Edgar, her *darling Eddie*,
had been dead for sixteen years, but nothing seemed to have
changed since he went. *Lord help my poor soul*, he'd said just
before he died in some room, some doorway, some Baltimore
street—sixteen years he'd been Old Line dust, and here she
was, begging yet. It was as though she didn't know, hadn't
been told, as though he were still in her care, ill or drugged
or sodden, *not himself*, as she'd written to Lowell—and after
sixteen years, she was making the same supplicant rounds

with the same yawning basket, still, in widow's cap and weeds, pleading for the swill that belonged to the dogs.

She was aged now, bereft so often that she was half-crazed, but in her mind, the half that was left, she was the mother-in-law, more, the mother of poor-devil Eddie as before. Sixteen years gone, he was nonetheless part of her household of paralytics and consumptives, of stuffed birds, caged birds, and the cat Catarina, still there in its stale chill, its smell of blood and bummed cuisines—and she, she was washing, nursing, sewing, running errands, dunning all and sundry, and waiting for someone's death, on the way and quickly coming. Whose?, she may have wondered as she mended clothes, mended mends, as she attended darling Eddie at some alehouse, waited outside in the dark, the rain. Whose death?, as she wrote to get him excused, *Dear Eddie's health was so bad, no, he could not get down to the office.* Whose?, as she borrowed and pawned to keep him out of jail, the piano (Virginia's piano!), the hair sofa, the chair set, the brown china (china for fair!) with its scenes of a Chinese river. Whose?, the day she lacked the carfare to go out begging.

God knows how she stood the pain of sight, seeing Virginia's hemorrhages, bright and gushing scarves for the bodice of her dress, how she bore the dearth of her board, the almost clean slate her dying family ate from, how she lived with death roundabout, in the next room, and sometimes in her arms. God knows how she lasted till no one needed her— and now she was in need ($5 *or even* three), and God knows whether she got what she asked for. If so, she may have bought something and taken it home to Eddie: in the good half of her mind, she may have thought he still was there.

Talahina Houston, 1795(?)–1838

TO HIS SQUAW IN INDIAN TERRITORY

I have made for you a kingdom.
            —Sam Houston, from Texas

She'd been seventy years in the ground when her unmarked grave was found near a small grove of cedars. It was
the stance of the trees, their chance formation, that recalled
the site to someone's mind, and when a growth of brush was
cleared away, there came to light a weathered mound. At no
great distance down, a broken set of bones was reached, those
of the leg and arm, two parts of a skull, and some few teeth,
white still, timeproof, sound; among this residue lay a comb
of tortoise-shell and a handmade sixpenny nail. The comb,
the nail, and the bones, together with their cushion of
kindred dust, all this was boxed and borne to Fort Gibson,
and there, on a day of rain, it was buried in the Officers' Circle, where the flag flew above the braid beneath the lawn.
Lost no more, the Cherokee—the bones were she, Talahina,
and hers the comb, the coffin nail.

Very little is known of her life, and but for having been a
governor's wife, the little might be less, be guesswork. There
are no likenesses of her—she died before Daguerre—and
since her mark appears but once, an X, even the spelling of
her name is moot, and it comes in fifteen ways. In telling of
her, though, all agree that when Houston saw her for the first
time—it was at the Green Corn rites—he was so taken by her
face and form that he followed her about for days, to the
week-long Penitentials, to the dancings and the stickball
games, and when it was not enough to view her from afar, he
drew closer: he married her.

It mattered to no one that he already had a wife, a white
woman named Eliza Allen: they'd split the blanket and dwelt
apart, and among the Indians, the Indian marriage took,
though not for life nor even long. It lasted two years, three,
four at most, but none looked for more, least of all Talahina—

33

or was it Tenia, Tiana, Titania, or one of the eleven other names she sometimes wore? By then, she knew the Governor well (the Big Drunk, he was called), and well too she knew why he'd given up Tennessee for dice and swill, become, like her, a Cherokee. The reason was white Eliza and whatever he'd charged her with on their wedding night. God knows what he said then, for neither ever told, but it made her quit his bed, and soon he was pissing low-grade whiskey. *There is a dreadful stir about our governor*, someone wrote. *He was married and is now parted from his wife. There is a thousand diferent tails afloat.*

Standing Bear, he'd named himself, declaring *I am a citizen of the Cherokee Nation*, but Talahina knew that he was no more Indian than the Nazareth Jew: he had white skin, and he was white within, and he'd gaze and gaze at the Texas road till she could see his day of going coming while it was still a far cry off. They say she rode with him part of the way to Texas, across the Arkansas and maybe even the Canadian, and then, wherever it was, she left him. They say too that in time he sent back a runner bearing a message: *I have made for you a kingdom.* But she had her kingdom, and she knew that the one he'd made was for himself, and she sent the runner away.

She was seventy years dead when her unmarked grave was found among the cedars, and from it certain bones were taken, and a tortoise-shell comb, and a sixpenny nail.

Molly Maguire, (?)–(?)

IMMIGRANT FROM THE EMERALD ISLE

Let the toast go merrily round,
Let Irish hearts conspire:
Tyrant hounds will be crushed down
By matchless Molly Maguire!
                    —Ribbonmen's song, c. 1845

No one really knew her there, not even those who raised
her a glass in Cork or Kerry, praised her in Ballymena. No
man had ever seen her face, none could state her age, her
place of birth, her parish, and none could say for sure from
whom she took the wafer. Some held her to have aged with
the years, a mortal grown feeble, helpless, and not a little
mad; and others supposed her always old, the very crone of
legend; but full many there were who swore to this, that she
was a young widow, poor and put upon, and that under her
whistling skirts, she wore a pair of pistols warm against her
thighs. The last was the drink that disguised the mind: there
she was, her white face growing dreams of the cream her
black dress hid, and there wasn't a boyo with bollocks that
didn't toss himself off when he thought her up in bed. Ah,
but she was a willing and hearty girl, that Molly, one to love
for her killing ways. And she killed, she did, like the mother
of all murder! She'd take a life as she'd take a piss—landlords,
agents, grippers, keepers, soldiers of the cold-ass Queen,
anything orange.

After the Famine, she came to Pennsylvania—some killing was needed in the coalfields—and they missed her in the
bogs she'd left behind, missed their fine damn Molly. It's
been a hundred years since she was heard of last, here or
there or anywhere else, but she'll be back some day, never
fear, and we'll see her flip her skirts and show that pair of
pistols, black, black as the hair between her thighs. She'll
come back. We'll see her. . . .

Margaret Fuller, 1810–50

THE BLUESTOCKING

I understand more and more of the character
of the tribes.

—Margaret Fuller

Rising six, she could render Latin at sight, the Gallic and
Civil Wars, Virgil, Horace, the *Metamorphoses*, and in its
cadences, in its power and precision, she'd hold forth on
bread, God, and J. Q. Adams as though no one had told her
the language was dead. And in damsel days, her fare was Cer-
vantes for his pratfall chivalry and Molière for the pungent
lunges of his wit, and the Bard, of course, she had by heart
before she knew the curse. At Mr. Perkins's school, she rose
at five and studied Greek and when free composed epistles
that disposed of Milton, Epictetus, and Racine. She paid for
such attainments with dreams of spectres, great faces coming
toward her, staring worlds, they seemed to be, and there
were trees that bled and raring horses, and she'd scream herself awake, or, still enwound with sleep, she'd roam the halls
and moan till someone found her.

All who knew her called her plain. She had light hair,
they say, and much of it, and in that day of snags and disen-
cumbered gums, her teeth were reckoned fine. Her prize fea-
ture was her eyes, bright, large, long-lashed, and often slit-
ted, and they could almost be seen in the act of seeing, as if
they almost flashed. Her talk was deemed the best of her age,
far-faring, many-tongued, and spangled, but nothing—talk,
teeth, or eyes—made the world unmindful: she was plain.

She had to settle for spiritual *deliciae*, and at thirty-five
she was still kissing and coupling in the unsprung bed of the
soul. What rare ones, though, she shared it with! Sages, some
were, and scholars, and divines, and one who proved what
not at Walden, and there were movers, shakers, cloud-com-
pellers, and many who merely thought out loud. For thirty-
five years, she was a fruitful brain unlearned in love, a fallow

36

know-it-all (or all things but one), and then she flew too near the sun and burned.

He was a Jew, her sun, a blue-eyed German, fluent, shrewd, a commission merchant, a buyer of something in the morning and a seller of something in the afternoon, a man of common sense, he was, unmoved by her uncommon mind, a common man. Nathan was his name, and he came from Holstein. Whatever she may have bestowed on him, a few mittened fingers or the whole naked works, she kept little out of her letters to him, and she wrote in such close symbols as *the first painful turnings of the key*. She must've alarmed him, either with her words or her thirty-five unlocked years: he withdrew, her Jew; he set, her sun.

When asked to return the letters (fellow! knave! shitepoke!), he put a price on them, whereupon she whose door had turned *on its golden hinge* made a note on the character of the *tribes*. Forgotten the rhythms of Ovid, the simple sequences of Caesar, forgotten the high mind, the immaterial life, the littleness of things—and because a beggarly Jew had bargained for a beggarly few per cent, the twelve tribes of Israel stood condemned. *I understand more and more*, she claimed, but for all her store of learning, there was no blue in her blood, only in her stockings and her nose.

Emma Crockett, 1857–(?)

IN ALABAMA, AT THE AGE OF EIGHTY

*I ain't scared of nothing.**
—Emma Crockett, ex-slave

She was four when the War began and fourscore when she spoke her one remembered line: *I ain't scared of nothing*, she said—no more is known. But there below her likeness, the words seem to smoke, to smolder, cinders to be stoked (it's a picture of heat!), and the sun makes a glowing place on

37

her skin, or is the sun within her and showing through her face? *I ain't scared of nothing,* she said, and to know what she was saying, she must've seen it all.

She was a child when the War came and still a child when it went, but she'd lived an eight-year lifetime, grown old, before they told her she was free, and by then, what was left to fear? She'd seen bucks on their knees to overseers, seen whips worn out on Catos and Mingos swing from trees. She knew what wenches weekly served the Master, and she knew their babies too, till they came up with the bucket from a well. And she'd met conjure-men and bought their conjure-things (*wrop 'em in a rag and tie 'em with a hair, two from a hoss and one from a mare*), and, mumbledy-mumbledy, she'd wished on them for wings. She'd heard preachy-preach, *don't steal, and you get to be a house-nigger in heaven,* but she preferred the speech of turkey-hens, and when they said *we poor, we poor,* she said *we poor account of the rich.* At eight, ah God!, she must've seen it all.

She's sitting on the top step of a three-step stoop, with one arm akimbo and the other at her side. Dressed in gingham, she wears an apron tied to her waist, and it glares, white and unrelenting, at the lens. She glares too, black and unrelenting—*I ain't scared of nothing,* she says, and there are the words, printed at her feet.

*Photograph and caption from *Lay My Burden Down*, B. A. Botkin, ed. (University of Chicago Press, 1945).

Evangeline St. Clare, in *Uncle Tom's Cabin* (1852)

LITTLE EVA: A GENRE PAINTING

She moved as in a happy dream.
> —Harriet Beecher Stowe

She's five or six when seen at first, an aerial being, graceful as steam. Golden brown her hair, we're told, and violet-blue her eyes, and though always dressed in white, she never seems to soil, as if, made of mist, she merely trails across this world, touching but untouched, and soon, like a thought fading, she'll come to naught and die. She's a picture made to move, paint somehow occurring, instancy prolonged. She has no form or color, though, no vitals of her own: she's merely acted-on pigment, and she flows, and the wonder is that she dies of lungs whose lights were Mrs. Stowe's.

Polly Ann Henry, (?)–(?)

JOHN HENRY HAD A LITTLE WOMAN

Her name was Polly Ann.
—ballad

It was Lucy Ann as well, and it was Julie Ann, and Ida Red, and Polly spelled in fourteen ways—it was even Mary Magdalene. But I was only John Henry's woman, and though in their songs, they sang *Where did you get them shoes you wear, the dresses that look so fine?*, they never took the trouble to memorize my name. All those tales they told in music, tall tales and true, and nobody knows my name!

They know, they say, where John was born, and they know where he was raised, but nary a one can tell if it was red I wore or blue. They know what he said on his pappa's knee—*A hammer be the death of me*—they know he went to the mountain and hammered till half past three. They know he drove fifteen feet to the steam-drill's nine in the Big Bend tunnel of the C. & O. line, and when he said *Hammer be the death of me*, he spoke true and soon fell dead, pore boy. But nobody knows if it was red I wore or blue.

Everybody knows the drill started out at half past twelve, and John didn't start till one, and they full well know that John bottomed out at half past three, and the drill wasn't done till four—pore drill! He won, John did, but he lost his life, for he died right there with the hammer in his hand—*hammer be the death of me*, he said, and it was. The whole world

39

knows such things, but no one saw the clothes I wore, the dress I got from a miner in a mine, the high-top shoes from a railroad man. *Never wear black, wear blue,* John once said, but nobody knows what color I wore, black or blue or red.

Woman posing, unidentified, 1859

PRINT FROM A WET-PLATE NEGATIVE

Statuary, she seems to be, a bust on a plinth of skirts, and from carven eyes, she stares past the camera at a man, or perhaps at another woman, behind the camera's back. In the picture, the light seems to be going, as if time were still running there and the hour growing late. A private place, that collodion world, posted, reserved, forbidding but somehow not quite forbidden, and at any moment, the man outside may enter it, or perhaps the other woman.

[From an unidentified photograph.]

Clara Albers, 1859

SMALL GRAVE ON THE GREAT PLAINS

Clara Albers
Born here 16 May 1859
Died here 16 May 1859

It's marked off, in a bounding main of wheat, by a free and easy fence of stones, thrown, they seem, instead of placed, a rough border for a mound now nearly gone. Catchall for trash from the air, for drifting spores, ash, winnowed chaff, worn by winds and the rain, tamped down by birds, mice, moles, worked on, wormed, by the four hundred seasons of a century, the tomb of Clara Albers has failed away to a round in a groundswell of wheat. Begun and done for on the same day, she's merely a name for a pinch or two of chemicals, all that remains of her blood, her brains, her extensible bones: she hardly lived at all.

But even so, she's there yet, a spoonful of earth, a trifle that trips the mind. Where had she been brought from, to be born here beside this future road, and where would she have gone if here she hadn't died? How long would she have lasted somewhere else, what would she have known, what good or evil done, what wonders seen or dreamed? And at the end, would she have rejoiced that she'd lived long or wished herself back to this, the one-day life that lay beneath the wheat?

Isabel Banford, in *Pierre, or The Ambiguities* (1852)

THY SISTER, ISABEL

Where a beautiful woman is, there is all Asia and her bazaars.
> —Herman Melville

It begins, this tale, on a summer morning so still that the earth, as though entranced by itself, seems to be holding its breath. It begins, on a green and golden day, with a swain (bright Pierre, his Lucy calls him) on the way to where his sun is rising, the *luces* in his Lucy's eyes: in her, he swears, *the skies do ope.* Into this void of serenity, a huggermugger missive comes, and though green and gold the tale has begun, there, at the beginning, the tale has begun to end. From the empyrean down, down through mortal sin to the fire underground, the hell of sister Isabel: in her, alas, the skies do lower.

Thy sister, she signs her covert screed, and he'd longed for one so long (*of all things, would to heaven I had a sister!*) that he takes her at her word. That shriek of hers when first she saw him, that Delphic burst, how could he doubt that her blood had cried out, and that his own had heard it? *Thou art*

41

not the only child of thy father, she writes; *the hand that traces this is thy sister's*—and thereupon the lights of Lucy start to fade, and the night sets in.

Bright Pierre no more, but dim now, dark Pierre, he goes to where his sister dwells, along some rude road through a vaulted wood, a place of stained-glass presences, drifting vapors, and in the groined gloom, she tells him how their currents came to join. The chronicle is of a childhood spent in the dusk, of dire solitudes, impending trees, a Grimm childhood in a stone and crumbling ruins, Chillon itself, it might've been. No mother can she recall, only an old man and woman who spoke to her but little, like gaolers—their faces were black with age, she says, the man's a purse of wrinkles.

She talks on, sister Isabel, she tells the early years away, and they pass, grotesque and doomful, a conjuration ill lit and involute, and though faces and places change, they go from strange to stranger still, until (she was nine or ten at the time) someone called her beautiful, and the word *Father* was said, and he who wore it embraced her, kissed her, glowed. But in no long while, another word wed it—*dead*, it was, and her joy died with it. The sister speaks, of intimations now, misted recollections, parts of names, a guitar that seemed to play by itself, to murmur in her ear, and now her half-world wander begins—water is crossed, she remembers—and she finds her way from a there unknown to Pierre! to here!

But somewhere in that telling, the bar of blood is broken, and what she'd sought as a sister, she finds as a flame, and thenceforth the way matters not to them, lonely though it be, lackluster, dread to the black end of life. He calls her wife, and straightway down they wend in flight, down, down through spite and hunger, through the hard cities of guilt, fear, despair, failure, down through murder and the brandished hands of the world to death by poison, not in some bazaar of Asia, but deep in a Manhatto dungeon.

Harriet Beecher Stowe, 1811–96

THE LORD HIMSELF WROTE IT

I was but an instrument in His hand.
—Harriet Beecher Stowe

Many an abomination has been laid at my door. Every clerk that rhymes on Sunday, every Rialto scrivener, every hack with the scribbling itch—all say that if they've sinned in words, they've sinned as me. Their sprung and stumbling rhythms, their daring dimmed by quotes, their Eureka!s among the known, their slow-motion wit—all declare these doings mine and doubt meanwhile my one Creation.

I didn't write this book, and I didn't use the woman as my fist. The fact is, I gave up writing a long way back, at the height of my powers and ahead of my time. Few read the stones I sent from Sinai and fewer my writ on the Chaldean wall, and all those few were Jews. Allow me this, though, that I used no blind; the name I signed was my own. Why hide now, then? And with the whole wide world to choose from, why behind a mother of seven, the wife of a crammer in Maine?

Her household smelled of smelling salts, of six children (I took back the seventh, a year-old boy), of tansy, camphor, bacon smoke, bound sermons, hand-me-down air, and, still faint and still afar, Bright's disease. I glanced through a window once and saw Mister conning the Scriptures and Missus dashing off a war, and the sight sent me home with the blues.

I never wanted that war (I didn't care a sneeze for the niggers), but she did, and she got it, and some five hundred thousand whites died for a book (in paper, cloth, or cloth full gilt, with discount to the trade). The only book that made more killing is the one that was written about me.

Mary Lincoln, 1818–82

GOOD FRIDAY AT FORD'S THEATRE

Mr. Lincoln is to be President of the United States some day. If I had not thought so, I would not have married him, for you can see he is not pretty.
— Mary Lincoln

He'd die the next morning, in the Peterson house across the street, but she'd beat about the world for another seventeen years before she lit and lay down beside him on that hill in Illinois. It'd be the same shot, though, that did for both of them, him in a matter of hours, her a long road later and hard going every yard of the way.

She was an odd make, God knows, a pustule of a woman, a sty, a sore, and you could hurt her with a word too many, one too few, or none at all, with a bow more curt than she thought her due. A cough out of season, a glance, sass, soft soap, even, and she'd storm you to shame though your name was Abe. She was vain of her blood, a rare vintage, she deemed it, claret from a peerless year. It galled her to be on the sawed-off side, squat, she seemed, and it served her not to put on airs: her feet still touched the ground. A short blue in the tall grass, she was, a better among worse, and with feuds outnumbering friends, she became a pigeon for her image in the glass: she bought six hundred pairs of gloves, shawls that cost in the thousands, pearls, diamonds, gowns, feather and ribbon bravery, traps, stuff, things, bought till buying alone was the end she sought. Still and all, money was her one and panic dream, money or its lack, and the shadow cast by plenty assumed the shape of need. She hearkened to diviners, to readers of signs, bell-ringers, beaters of drums in the dark. She was a nest of whims and pique, of spleen and dander, and a fire always smoldered in her grate. She was a suite of ills and pain, with chambers for chills and fevers, for the migraine, the uterine lesion, and a curse that came in spates, and before the finish there'd be fluid in her tissues,

44

sugared urine, swellings of the hand and foot, and she'd suffer loss of weight, failing vision, an impairment of the mind, a fall from a chair. . . .

A long road hers, and she'd die it by the inch. She'd have little at the last—a pair or two of those gloves, some rags of *mousseline de soie*, a torn fan, a balding fur, no friend, no feud, and one damn son who'd sworn her mad. And yet, what would she have done to be brought so low—lived near the light and not been lit? Would that be her crime, that she'd never glowed, that she'd lowered Abe's day with her night?

Mrs. Mary Surratt, 1820(?)–65

A HANGING: four exposures

Don't let me fall!
—Mary Surratt

1

From the copestones of a brick wall, twenty-eight Federal soldiers, one squatting, three sitting, and all at ease, gaze at a gallows in the weeds and footworn grass below. The platform is bare save for two pairs of facing chairs, and these seem less to be seats than seated there and staring each other down. The July day is hot, and on the ground in a block of shade the hangmen stand, one in a black silk hat and one with hat in hand.

2

The soldiers are on their feet now, but not yet at attention; some of them lounge, embracing their bayonets, and some lean against a rope ratline strung along the wall. Below them, the platform is crowded with officials, witnesses, and the four about to die. Though the July day is hot, only one of the four, the woman, is shielded from the sun. Off in a corner, a chevroned sergeant stands to his gun: a spare umbrella.

45

3

The hoods are going on and the ties for knee and ankle,
and five umbrellas can now be seen, but none between the
sun and the doomed. The July day is hot, and for them the
way will not be long. *Don't let me fall!* the woman said.

4

But she did fall, along with the other three, and all four
hang still. Only a dozen soldiers remain on the wall, and of
these some are blurs, men in motion, going, and down below
the crowd goes too. Soon none but the four will be left, somewhere between the vacant platform (where are the chairs?)
and the hot and trodden yard.

[From photographs by Alexander Gardner, 1865.]

Mrs. George Armstrong Custer, 1842–1933

I DREAMED OF YOU

Oh, Autie, we must die together!
—Elizabeth Bacon Custer

She saw the expedition off at Fort Abraham Lincoln—
seventeen hundred animals, there were, and twelve hundred
men, and what with wagons, pack mules, and artillery, the
train was strung out two miles long, and over the Dakota
plain, it raised a cloud of dust that hung all day in the late-
May air. It was there again, or still, in the morning, rarer in
the distance than before and lower to the ground, but it was
there—she could see it from her door. There were other
women at other doors, she noticed, where the officers lived
and in Laundress Row, and they too gazed at the brown haze
against the basement of the sky.

In her mind as well, there was a kind of cloud, a slow
commotion, smoke, it might've been, fine as a phantom,
something to be waved away. The post was quiet that day,

46

palpitant, it seemed to be, as if she were listening to herself living, and expectant, as of the coming sound of guns. *Autie,* she sometimes called her General, and sometimes she called him *Bo*—and when she found herself thinking *Autie, we must die together!*, she tried to brush free of the thought, the ghost, but now it was partly real and inside her head to stay.

Drawn for some reason to the General's study, she made a tour with her eyes of the papered room. The pattern was a small figure set in diagonals, a sprig of color that climbed and descended the walls, and whatever was seen against it also seemed to move. The racks suspended from the molding, the military gear, the books, the photographs, all were insecure, and so too the antlers above the table, the snowy owl, the pronghorn heads, the picture of a woman in a wedding gown—*white rep silk with trail,* she thought, *bertha of point lace, embroidered blossoms on the brow of the veil. . . .*

The map of the western territories, the binocular case, the forage cap, the training manuals, her glance passed from each of these slowly, as if she were committing their shape and condition to memory—the crease that crossed the Rockies, the pushpins along the Yellowstone, the stains, the scuffed leather—and faintly from somewhere (the map, was it, or the world outside?) came the sound she knew she'd been waiting for: firing. *Oh, Autie,* she thought, *we must die together!*

But they didn't. Six weeks later, with two hundred and sixty-four soldiers, couriers, and interpreters, one of them black, with Bloody Knife and two dozen Arikara scouts, with horses, mules, six Crows, and the guide Lonesome Charley Reynolds, Autie died on a gentle slope leading down to the Little Big Horn. She lived for another fifty-seven years.

Lydia Hamilton Smith, 1813–84

HOUSEKEEPER OF THADDEUS STEVENS

No man has been charged with more vices than I have.
　　　　　　　　　　　　　　　　—Thaddeus Stevens

　　One such vice was the quadroon widow of a black barber (some say carpenter), and when she went to work for the club-footed congressman, she was thirty-five years old, light gold, a Creole sparkler. It was her mixed blood that grew her so, lined her skin with colored silk, modified its tone, emulsified it, made it a milk of precious stones. She was two decades in that household, and those by whom she was seen there, guests, tradesmen, all affirmed that she bore herself well, spoke seldom and then with point, wore clothes that were clean and seemly: by no sign, they said, was she Stevens' whore. In Lancaster, though, no one thought her otherwise, and when he brought her to Washington, there too the rumor ran, and her discretion, her self-effacement, poise, reserve, the care she used, her sense of place, even her Romanist attachment, lifelong and faithful, all these merely embellished belief: she was a Mariolatrous whore. In death, she was the Virgin's still, being buried in St. Mary's Catholic Cemetery under a stone that called her *the trusted housekeeper of Honorable Thaddeus Stevens*. Was that the fact, or was she really . . . but why should it matter? What difference does it make?

Margaret Carrington, 1831–70

EXPEDITION TO ABSARAKA

The land should bear its true name.
—Margaret Carrington, 1868

To her, the country north and west of the Platte had always been Absaraka, always the Home of the Crows, and it mattered not that others had chosen to call it Wyoming, a place name meaning plains: all through her journal, it was Absaraka, and it ran from the Platte to the Yellowstone. *A precious region to the Indians*, she wrote, and note was made of wild wheat in profusion, of grass so dense as to slow a running horse, and game abounded there, she said, deer in droves dwelt among the pines and the box elder, in the groves of ash, and there were grapes, there were plums and cherries numberless, and rife such riches as the hare, the sage hen, the cinnamon bear, and even as buffalo herds hid the earth at times, so did birds the sky. It was good, the Crows would say, *Wash-ta-la!* their Absaraka, and they were evil who would take it away—*Wan-nee-chee!*

> Chief Red Cloud to Colonel Carrington: I and my people
> will fight you. We will kill every white man who crosses
> the Crazy Woman's Fork of the Powder River!

But the expedition had been ordered by General Pope (*I don't care for John Pope a pinch of owl-shit*, someone once had said), and, seven hundred strong, it set out from Fort Kearney on a march toward Bozeman, far beyond Crazy Woman's Fork. The train was two hundred and twenty mule-teams long, and the wagons bore women and families and mowing machines, doors, sashes, and sewing chairs, locks, glass, kegs of nails, turkeys, canned fruits, howitzers, churns, and a brace of swine. In the van, between his guidons, rode Colonel Carrington. His wife was two miles back, part of the stirred-up dust.

> Chief Red Cloud to Colonel Carrington: As long as I live
> I will fight for the last hunting grounds of my people!

He and his people fought all the way to the Big Horns. They attacked, with great vigor, fifty-one times, and ninety-one soldiers and five officers died as promised on the road to Montana. Most of these were killed, as the journal relates, in the course of a single day along Lodge Trail Ridge just beyond Crazy Woman's Fork. There, on the twenty-first of September, 1866, Captains Fetterman and Brown, Lieutenant Grummond, and seventy-six soldiers of the 18th U.S. Infantry and 2nd U.S. Cavalry were cut off a few miles from their fort and slain to a man.

Colonel Carrington's report to the Adjutant General at Omaha was appended to his wife's journal, and in part it read as follows:

> . . . I was asked to send all the bad news; I do it so far as I can. I give some of the facts as to my men, whose bodies I found just at dark, viz.: Eyes torn out and laid on the rocks; noses cut off; ears cut off, chins hewn off; teeth chopped out; joints of fingers; brains taken out and placed on rocks with other members of the body; entrails taken out and exposed; hands cut off; feet cut off; arms taken out from sockets; private parts severed and indecently placed on the person; eyes, ears, mouth and arms penetrated with spear-heads, sticks, and arrows; ribs slashed to separation with knives; skulls severed in every form, from chin to crown; muscles of calves, thighs, stomach, breast, back, arms and cheek taken out. . . .

Truly, as she said in her journal, truly it was a precious region to the Indians!

Mrs. Henry Adams, 1843–85

HOODED FIGURE

"Henry, I do wish you would marry Clover Hooper."
"Heavens, no! They're all as crazy as coots. She'll
kill herself."
—Charles Francis Adams, Jr., *Memorabilia*

And yet, as his mother had wished, Henry did marry
Clover. And as his brother had predicted, she did kill herself.
She drank pyrogallic acid, the developing fluid, a bitter and
caustic phenol, and she was dead in less than an hour, gone
when he found her on the floor before the fire. Little more is
known of that Sunday afternoon: only they were in the house
at the time, and soon he was there alone. All the Hoopers
were crazy, Charles had said, and he may have wandered,
wondering, from that vinegar beginning to this corrosive end.
He may have thought of their wedding trip, of the rose windows of another world, the lichens, the lakes, the tinted Tus-
can towns, two years of drift—and he may have remembered
how the end began on the Nile. It was there that she'd become dull, dependent, cast down (*they're all as crazy as
coots*), there that he'd sensed, almost seen, what was still far
off. It took her thirteen years of Sundays—the late breakfast,
the light talk, the void ahead, the night—thirteen years to
excuse herself, climb a flight of stairs, and die of inner burning before a fire on the floor. No more Sundays, she may have
thought, and she was dead.

Where he buried her, he caused a monument to be
placed, a block of granite with egg-and-dart molding below a
chaste cornice; against this in bronze, a caped and cowled
figure seated on a rough-hewn dolmen. Often, in the thirty-
odd years that were left of his life, he'd come here to gaze at
the peppered stone, the pebbled cope, the hooded figure's
hooded eyes. But the memorial would tell him nothing, not
even its name, would not let him in—and it was *his* dream-
up, *his* design! At such times, he'd turn back to ransack him-

self, to seek inside what only Clover had brought to light, seen somehow with her darkened mind. He never found it. He never knew why she'd excused herself that Sunday morning, gone upstairs, and died.

Mrs. Cornelia Clinch Stewart, 1802–86

THE MERCHANT AS MERCHANDISE

A. T. Stewart, the merchant prince, has presented Mrs. Abraham Lincoln with a love of a shawl, valued at. . . .
—a New York paper

They say he'd buy up stock at failures and fire auctions, and his wages were lower than the going rate and his prices higher, and he'd fine his clerks for breaking rules, a dime for coming late, two bits for being rude, and when the size of a purchase pleased him, he was known to throw in a prize, a ribbon, a paper of pins, a buttoncard, a little for a lot. The hard and careful mick, that's how he got his forty millions, his eight-story emporium, his silk and cotton and carpet mills, his marble pile on Fifth, and his *things*, his land and bonds and tenements, one such the Grand Union at Saratoga Springs. What he did not get, of course, was eternal life in those endless aisles of his, immortality in his eight-floor Kingdom of Trash. He died at seventy-three, still *comme il faut* for the clientele, still hell on wheels for the staff. He had to leave all that gallantry behind him, all those fines he meant to levy and the notions he had in mind for Mesdames: forty millions went off like forty cents.

At his desire, he was buried at St. Mark's, just around the corner from the store, as if even in the grave he intended to drive hard bargains, nail tardy arrivals, watch skirts turn flirtsome in the wind, and for a time perhaps he did preside from the other side of Here, a ghastly prince of tradesmen, a counter-jumping ghost. . . . And then ghouls stole him out of the churchyard, stole the box that held his bones, the horn on his toes and fingers, and his once-worn suit of clothes, stole him, a secondhand man in serge, stained by seeping rain, faded, out of style, goods that would never sell—and offered him for sale.

Twenty thousand, they asked his widow for the article, a love of a cadaver despite the jelly eyeballs, the loosening teeth, the hair grown after the funerary shave—oh, a love, it was, and at twenty thou' a steal. Cornelia haggled for two years, and by then the eyes were gone altogether, and the teeth had fallen through the brainless skull, and the suit of serge was succumbing to rust. Soon, she must've thought, Mr. Stewart would be lost. There was less of him now, she argued in a try at cutting the cost, but twenty was the figure, and that's what she paid in the end.

Statue of Liberty, 1886 –

A MIGHTY WOMAN WITH A TORCH
as seen from Ellis Island

Give me your tired, your poor,
Your huddled masses . . .
                                    —Emma Lazarus

A boat's-length away from the dock, a half-sunk ferry squats on the bottom between two piers. Her nameboard is gone from the wheelhouse (the *Wm. Fletcher*, was she once, or was she the *John K. Moore?*), and missing too her walking beam, and her empty davits lean and listen (to whom, and what language do they hear?). Tides have marked their highs on her woodwork, and like the stream beyond, her buckled decks ripple. How near she came (the *Magnolia?* the *Patrol?*) before going down, only a boat's-length away from the tired, the poor, and they within sight of the golden door!

The ferry slip has been worked on by the weathers of a century. The drawbridge, for drays and passengers once, has fallen from its hoist, and these days it slants downward, leads down to the bay. The stringers have rotted to shatters of punk, and the planks have split in the dry and damp of sun and rain. The ramp leads only to the water now, and where it goes under, there the eel-grass grows, long green hair that rises, falls, flows with the eddies.

Beyond all this molder, all these losses to luck and rust, between a simmer of river and a steam of sky, the Genetrix—afloat in the vapor, vaporous too, the Mother of Exiles! From here, she's an endless undulation, like the run around her feet: her seams cannot be seen, nor the rivets in her face and gown, nor can her verdigreen. From here, she's dreamspun still, still beckoning all the world.

The empty davits lean and listen, and on the worn timbers, the sound of bygone feet is heard, *the huddled masses*, and they pound, the *homeless, the tempest-tost*, and into the waters they go, all those millions, down, down, and disappear, *wretched refuse*, like these splinters here, that foundered ferry.

[From a photograph by John Veltri, 1970.]

Emily Dickinson, 1830–86

REVENGE OF THE NERVES

> . . . *the doctor calls it.*
> —Emily Dickinson

A sickbed phrase, garish words for pallid days, but in his journal he wrote *Bright's disease*. From a long-sunk Anatomy, some bubbles of lore still rose, and on a remembered renal section, he saw the Malpighian pyramids, the columns of Bertin—*Bright's disease*, he thought, and he reached for a pen, but the pen was in his hand and his finding on the page. He knew what was killing her, and he could almost set the time. He knew from the color and kind of urine, from the pains in the back, the fever, the hydroptic hands and feet, he knew from old books, old cadavers—*Bright's disease.*

It was a high wide world, the room she lay in, and the sights it held he never descried. There were wilds inside the wall, there were rare shores and private ports of call, and he strode unaware among flowers, flights of bees, birds achant in a virgin mode. In that world of hers, he breathed love, not air, but what he sought there was Bowman's capsule, and what he found was a name for death—*Bright's disease.*

Emma Lazarus, 1849–87

PERSONS THAT PASS

. . . shadows that remain.
—Emma Lazarus

Somewhere, in some Aryan history of the Jews, she came upon the old aspersion, that it was they who'd wrought the Black Death on true believers, who'd poisoned the wells and air, cast the spells, killed with incantations and the power of their eye—it was all the fault of the fall-guy Jews. For this, they were denied their lives, and when sent to the stake for their own black death, they cried out for a pyre with a floor above the fire, that they might do as Miriam did with her timbrel—dance—and, the boon granted, to some Jew tune they died.

Persons that pass, she wrote.

Maria Mitchell, 1819–89

THE REGION OF TRUTH

Just beyond the daily mist of our minds.
—Maria Mitchell

She couldn't sleep, not with the mesh of her transit broken, the reticule that checked the inclination of the stars. She couldn't forget the sweeps of the night before, the clear, the deep still sky, the nebulae in Leo, and then across her sight the hairs had given way—it was as if the earth itself had burst its meridians—and she'd make no more measurements until the net was mended. She lay awake, pondering how to repair it: of the collimating screws, which came first, she wondered, and, once she'd drawn the tube, which of those on the diaphragm, and then, that done, what was she to use for the crossing lines, the grid by which she read the courses, told the time?

When day came, she took hairs from her own head, *white ones*, she said, *because I have no black to spare*, and making a fix of wax, she stuck them to the frame, but all six dissolved in an alcohol wash, and the work (*nice ladylike work*, she called it) was begun again and twice more undone—she was at it all day—before the hairs held. *But fine as are the hairs of one's head*, she wrote in her journal, *I shall seek something finer*, and seeking, she found it. She remembered a cocoon she'd seen in the Atheneum, and she went there, and it was where she'd left it, undisturbed and still perfect, and with those ladylike hands of hers, she took it home and carefully unrolled it. A spider had spun the cords in which she'd snare the stars!

The delicacy, the patient pains, the precision! Small wonder that on the first of October, 1847, at half past ten o'clock, P.M., she discovered a telescopic comet nearly vertical above Polaris about five degrees, *just beyond the daily mist of our minds*.

56

Mrs. Herschel Gruenberg, 1870(?)–1947

AUNT SARAH

Turn none away from thy door, for, who can say? one day may come an angel.

—ancient wisdom

To eke out her husband's earnings as a house painter, she sorted and carded hair, wove it into wigs. In the evenings, seated beneath the little blue hand of a gas-jet, Herschel would cipher in a pocket-book—areas, prices, hours—and Sarah would strand and wreathe her retes of hair. They were newly come to the American States, this pair from Kovno Guberniya, and being new as well to wedlock, they were, by the will of God, childless still. Let it be said at once that this condition was due to no lack of diligence. Nay, nightly or nearly so did they strive to breed a son—a son, please God, to sow their seed! But His ways were past their understanding, and, all praise to His name!, not yet had He blessed their union.

Each evening, as hitherto said, when ardor had ebbed, they repaired to the other room of the two-room flat, and there, beneath a flare of gas, Herschel summed his numbers, and Sarah wove her wigs. They spoke seldom at such times, but sound was all around them: a raucous faucet dripped, damp wood squibbed in the stove, and from the gas-pipe came a râle or rasp, a rhoncus, as though it were diseased. Aye, Herschel wrote and Sarah wrought, and so they spent their evenings, so a winter went, and not even then, sad to relate, were portents seen, the green blossoms of coming fruit.

On a certain night, an account of which is about to be given, all had gone according to usage: fervor had been followed by phlegm, and Herschel was again at his numbers and Sarah again at her wigs. And yet, though it seemed the same, the night was unlike any other night, and the difference lay in this: there was a knock on the door. No more than that—just a knock on the door—but great was the change it made. No one had knocked before.

The caller, when Sarah revealed him in the hallway, proved to be a man of uncertain years, ageless, some might have thought, but few would have doubted that his clothes, though frayed, were clean; indeed, from his person a zephyr of anise and cinnamon issued to invade the room. To the senses, then, the stranger seemed acceptable, but even so, when Sarah made as if to invite him in, Herschel frowned and shook his head. But that cold-water flat, that Lower East Side bower, was Sarah's domain, and within its walls her sway was feudal. She glared her husband's frown away and gestured for the stranger to enter.

Seating himself, the man nodded, now at Sarah and now at Herschel, nodded as at something said, but in truth nothing was said, and after many a moment nodding no longer annulled the void, and the stranger spoke, explaining his presence thuswise. He had received a letter, he said, and from it he had learned of the Gruenbergs, lately from the Old Country, and he had been told to pay them a visit: to do so would be a good deed, he had been assured, a *mitzvah*. He produced no letter, however, and he cited no names, wherefore his explanation, like his savor of spice and herb, was but a trifle on the air.

Turn none away, taught the wise of other days, and Sarah, wife of Herschel, heeded. She offered food now to the stranger, and when he pleaded surfeit—he had dined within the hour, he said, dined well—she pressed him, whereupon he acquiesced and ate. He ate—*Shema, Yisroel*, it was a marvel, the way he ate! He was a wonder at the work, a mentor so masterful as to stun the mind and stare the eye. Forsooth, his art was such that he hardly seemed to eat at all: ingesta simply vanished.

When the cupboards contained no more that was fit to serve, when only orts and rinds remained, the long repast ended. By then, Sarah and Herschel were in need of nothing so much as a night's repose, but for this boon their hopes were small. Nourished, the stranger had found his voice, and he was discoursing much as he had eaten, with no apparent end. He talked, he talked—*Shema, Yisroel*, he talked as though he held all tongues and of these he held all words!

Herschel, in the act of writing the area of a certain wall—77 square feet, it happened to be—fell asleep in his chair. Duty to the guest being drear but plain, Sarah continued to plait hair until her eyes refused the gift of sight, and, nudging Herschel, she took his place in Nod at once and mayhap used his dream. For a while, he cast up his columns again, that queer and serried army, and when he began to drowse, he roused Sarah, and then Sarah sat as he slumbered, after which she slept and he marshaled his numerous numbers—but always (*turn none away!*) one was awake to hear the stranger. And so the night was spent, and never the stranger stopped till the light of morning shone, and then quite suddenly he was gone, as though he had not been there.

He was not, of course, an angel. He was a teacher of Hebrew, Mendelson by name, Jacob Mendelson, and through the years often did he call on the Gruenbergs, and ever when he came he ate much though never hungry, and when he chose to speak—and he spoke!—one or another heard. They were blessed with many children, the Gruenbergs, but none of these was due to Mr. Mendelson. As already said, he was not an angel.

Mary Hallock Foote, 1847–1938

WOMAN BY THE TRAIN TRACKS

The emptiness of the sky by day is marvelously atoned for
by great nights of stars.
                              —Mary Hallock Foote, of the far West

Not quite marvelously enough: space stifled her all her
life. It's there in her letters to the East, that sense of trammel,
it's in her stories, her black-and-white sketches, it's unre-
deemed by the stars and nights. For her, there was no freedom in grandeur; grandeur bound her. Born on a farm in the
Hudson River valley, she grew up in a measured world and
knew its metes and monuments, but even so, she found room
there for her mind. The West, all vacancy and undefined distances, suppressed her.

Woman by the Train Tracks is a drawing she made for
one of her fictions, but she may well have been picturing herself; though it covers only half a page, it seems to tell her life.
The woman stands on a railway platform two steps up from
her gear, a stack of valises, boxes, canvas sacks. These lie beside a pair of rails running in a diagonal toward the horizon,
where a faint shading on the sky, a smear like an erasure, is
all that remains of a train: it had stopped, gotten rid of these
things, of the woman too, and gone. There, against immensity, she's something wrapped, a package no less than those at
her feet—she's surrounded by herself, and from within, with
expanses in all directions, she'll write small stories, draw pictures for half a page.

She'll remember her mother, in gray and lavender,
seated next to a belle in green and yellow, and she'll speak of
a cockatoo conversing with a wren. And she'll remember a
Catskill winter morning when *the sun just risen at our backs*
made our shadows all legs streaking ahead of us. And she'll
call the Mexicans of Almaden *the poor people of the sun,* and
of one who'd posed for her, she'll observe that he was hurt by

an offer of payment, and she'll record the national finality of his words: *No posíble!* She'll see things well, she'll write quietly, wear *a Holbein look of calm,* she'll dwell under great nights of stars, she'll be seemly and susceptive, she'll be small.

Maggie's Mother, in *Maggie* (1893)

LIKE A DEVIL ON A JAPANESE KITE

> *. . . her eyes a rolling glare . . .*
> —Stephen Crane

She curses the slum she lives in, the sty she's let it become, summons doom and demons down, as if she were not her own damnation. All succumbs to her, or to her drunken ghost—wood, glass, tin, plaster, all undone by her juniper fury, and in the tenemental gloom, the sound of smash can be heard. She alone seems to flourish there, and she glows, looms lurid and impending from the walls, *her eyes a rolling glare.*

Well, Mag's dead, she's told, and through a cud of bread, she says *Deh blazes she is!* Mag, on the turf and off so soon, dead in some doorway, gutter, gas-filled room, and a memory comes of her infant feet, so small, so small, *no bigger dan yer tumb,* and yet they'd grown to walk the streets! Peewee feet, *no bigger dan yer tumb,* the mother cries, and as she dwells on the peewee boots they'd worn, her eyes rain in remembrance. But it's a gin rain that falls, and only the weeds of hatred burgeon. The little feet, she thinks, the little worsted boots, and she says when someone pleads, *I'll fergive her! Oh, yes, I'll fergive her!*

Mrs. Theodore (Elizabeth) Tilton, 1835–97

A WORK OF THE FLESH

What a pretty house this is! I wish I lived here!
> —Rev. Henry Ward Beecher

In that fulsome age, she was small and meet, five feet tall
or less, it's said, and a hundred pounds in all, but a portrait
shows her ripened rounds, her curvatures in clothes. Black,
the dress she wore to sit for Mr. Page, black with a white lace
jabot, a white downfall—or uprise, since the flow as painted
is toward the face. A place of entrances, eyes that seem to
open inward, a mouth akin to the one between her thighs,
pale, the face, an oval invitation in a close embrace of hair.
What a pretty house!, the preacher said.

He said he wished to live there, but one already did,
Theodore his friend, adorant, well-nigh son, who, within that
satin and retentive hive, had begotten five on those occasions
when his mind stayed on its work. There were times, though,
when it strayed from the pink concaves of the pretty house to
his dearest friend, his idol, his almost-father—Beecher. By
date of birth, they were twenty years apart, the two, and yet
they weren't twain: in heart, in thought, in God, their source
of elevation, there were no divisions—except of course that
house, that house, wherein both might enter, but one was
forced to ring.

He rang, the preacher, once each day, the neighbors noticed, and in Theo's absence twice, and within he played with
the children and paid them bribes, he sat and sighed (*I wish
I lived here!*), and his afflation filled the lubric gloom. She,
her head bent over thread and thimble, sat and sewed for
baby-dollies while he rummaged her with his eyes, ransacked
her, and they murmured, she and her pastor, of God's love,
of walking in His spirit, of the sweet fruits of that spirit, joy,
peace, and a purity of mind in which all things were rendered
pure, and he mentioned (softly and as from some candescent
recess of his geist) the *oeuvre* he was writing—*Jesus Christ,*

a Life—and when she raised her glims and gazed at his, he knew that wishing was ended, that here he lived at last!

Days, then, of trysting notes, a come-and-go of cryptic embassies, and in them hours were set and places fixed, and the billets-doux held whispers of the last time and the frou-frou of the next. But prudence, the cold cone in their flame, told them to foresee the inopportune—a Theo, say, in rut in the afternoon—wherefore they'd arrange for a change of rendezvous or, if needs must, for lust deferred to a later day. But such fortuities were rare, and oft he tore her rose of skirts and kissed its core of hair.

Between them, she always claimed, there was only a love of God, a love that both felt toward Him and, through Him, for one another. A natural expression, it was, a joinder of the flesh that symbolized the unity of their souls with that of God, a holy thing and sinless, a Heaven here on earth. When Theo found out, though, there was hell to pay in Paradise.

He brought suit, the seeming son against the quasi father. The trial consumed six months, and when it was over, Theo had nothing to show for it but the cuckold's horn, and his wife was old at forty, gray, worn, and going blind, a house (pretty once) with the curtains drawn. The preacher never missed a tick or a tock. From the same pulpit, more wind, in the same pews, more women, and for another dozen years, he showed his flock the Way, some on a couch in the vestry and some in hansom cabs. He was so full of tuck that it took a stroke to stop him.

Mariana Andrada, 1830(?)–1902

· MARIANA *la loca*

These rocks that you see are not rocks. They are the three
temples that were lost at Galilee. . . .

—Crazy Mariana

No one can be sure it was she who, drunk and lurching,
came that day to the railroad tracks and, blind to the crossing
sign, stumbled onto the right-of-way. It might've been she,
though, she who was struck by the train, her blood that
stained the ties, her broken bottle of wine. Someone was
killed that afternoon five miles north of Hanford on the Santa
Fe line, and—who can tell now?—it may well have been *la
loca*, that crazy fandango dancer, up from Sonora to whore
among the Californios. Who can say now, who now knows?

Few the facts about her, and the farther back the more
obscure, as who her family were, what her class and actual
age. At a guess, she was twenty or so when first seen swirling
in the San Joaquin, a flame, they say, a flow of fire, and she
made men seek the shade, they say, as if she were the noon-
day sun. Her teeth, white and small, were simply a ceramic
marvel; her coloring, bright as burning, flashed; and the flex-
ions of her figure beckoned to the mind—so they say, but
quien sabe, who can find where truth lay, who can know the
lie? The widow of Murrieta, she called herself, but it's said
that she never saw him, that he was dead before her advent,
his head on display in alcohol. But some believed her all the
same, and to her whore appeal she added the bandit's fame,
and for another score of years, she danced the floors of *cantinas*, often on her back.

At forty, when her favors began to fail, there came to her
tidings of a certain Franciscan, one Fr. Magin Catala, a holy
man believed by the people to have healed the sick in miraculous fashion, and it was credited too that the Virgin—She
Herself!—had passed from his presence into three great rocks
in the western sierra. He was thought to be immortal, being

already nine hundred years old, and it was said that he dwelt among the very rocks where Our Lady had disappeared. . . . And from there, *la loca* now claimed, he spoke a spate to her ear alone. *By order of the Padre Magín,* she cried, *and by the power of the Almighty, this world is coming to an end, and I am here, sisters and brothers, to save you from the blazes of hell!*

They sold their goods, the sisters and brothers, and they brought her much money and many gifts, but the world did not come to an end as she'd foretold, and the simples that she'd simoned began to drift away. To hold them, she predicted for someone's child its ordained time of death—and she was right to the hour, for she'd poisoned it herself. The act could not be proved, but with the death of the child, the commune among the rocks ended, and so too communion with Padre Magín.

The years passed, the years passed, and here and there and now and then word was heard of *la loca* in the San Joaquin, at Idria, and Avenal, and Poco Chine, and at last one day, there was that dress that lay by the tracks, the jelly of blood and wine, and it may have been she, the whore, the dancer from Sonora, the disciple of Padre Magín. . . .

Kate Chopin, 1851–1904

A WALK TO THE GULF

I always feel sorry for women who don't like to walk; they miss so much.

—Kate Chopin

She died two days after a stroke had flooded her brain. No priest stood or knelt at her bedside and spoke of her soul to Jesus, no oils were felt by her eyes and ears, her hands and feet, or, seat of her passions, her reins. No oil of olives touched her, no fatness of oil, and therefore no plea went up

65

for her pain's easement. She had long since given over wearing the cross that in her early pictures lies on her breast, but it may have left its mark, a faint indentation, say, some place that seemed paler than the rest of her skin. A thin reason, but they buried her in ground that knew the grace of God. Odd, though, that no trace of her grave can be found today.

No trace as well of Mme. Pontellier, the self she put on paper, herself in words, her sentient personation, but quite as warm as she. Pontellier, she called her fiction, and the name, as it drifts through the flowered pages, gives off the flowers' flavor, camomile, pungent and acerb, as if some bitter herb were being breathed. White, she wears, and it sails her over the yellow blossoms and down across the beach. She stands near, watching the Gulf fluctuate like something in the making, watching its colors flash and fade, and she hears small waves whisper as they reach for her feet. *They miss so much*, she thinks, those women who do not walk. They sit, they sleep, secure in the clothes of stillness, and they never learn the secrets they keep from themselves; they're poised there, dressed for living, and living never comes. *They miss so much*, she thinks, and bare for once in the open air, she delights in the sun and invites the wind. *They miss so much*, she thinks, and she wades into the water and walks away from land.

Olivia Langdon Clemens, 1845–1904

A FALL ON THE ICE

She edited everything I wrote.
—Mark Twain

Her father dealt in coal, and she brought a mort of money to the marriage bed, a quarter of a million, it's said, but with the cash and the wife came her lifelong cachexia, a balance so unstable that a ray of light, a murmur, might disturb it. There was an imminence of debacle about her, the vapor, almost, of the little *mal*—she seemed to be breakable. At sixteen, she'd slipped and lost her footing—she'd been skating, climbing a stair, stepping from a sleigh—and when borne to a room, two years she lay unable to stir. She walked again only when a wizard conjured motion, but she was never really well to the end of her days: she was a mere equilibrium, and she dwelt in fear of a second fall.

When she said *change "breechclout"* and *take "offal" out*, when she said *some other word would be better than "stench,"* it was as if a command had come from an étagère—a milkglass hand had spoken, a porcelain figurine, the breakable thing that was not yet broken. But when he changed *"breechclout"* and took *"stench"* and *"offal"* out, it was he who broke. The second fall was his.

Louise Clappe (Dame Shirley), 1819–1906

LETTERS FROM THE CALIFORNIA MINES

It was a beautiful bird, a little larger than the domestic hen. . . .
—tenth letter, Nov. 25, 1851

She put in better than a year at the diggings along the North Fork of the Feather, and from Rich Bar and Indian Bar, she wrote twenty-three letters to her sister *in the states*. They were long, most of them, and nearly all spoke of gold, the sun that spun the world. They told of rockers, flumes, drifts, strange names for the places where those sunbeams might be found, told too of glints and gleams in long toms, races, tailings, and even underground. She reported on the rag-roofed houses, the sod floors, the twenty-nine physicians and the nine-and-twenty whores, and there was much about montemen, duels, and the acts of God called accidental, such as trees falling on people, gaunt redskins, fleas, drownings in the quagmire streets, and there were pages, pages about blue murder and bluer executions, butchering-bees, really, and amid famine for the lesser colors, there were feasts for the whites—oysters from the Bay and effervescent rain, champagne.

"Dame Shirley" was the name she gave herself in those twenty-three letters from the Rio de las Plumas about mules, Mexicans, amputations, profanity heard through calico walls— it was "Dame Shirley" calling a rattlesnake *a chain of living opals* and a lake *a wasted jewel*. But once, in the tenth letter, she saw and set down more than tropes, more than manners, mud, gangrene: in the death of a single bird, she saw two genders warring, saw the sexes' civil war.

The bird was a prairie hen, a *gallina del campo*, and her husband had trapped it in a coyote hole and brought it home alive. She wanted to free it (*I have resolutely refused to keep wild birds*, she wrote), but when her husband threatened to kill it for supper, she gave it the run of the cabin. It had a bright eye, she said, and though always shy of all, it seemed to delight in the curve of its plumes, even in their colors, *a somber mosaic*. Not for long, though: one day, with scarcely a sound, it shrank inside its feathers, fell down, died. The woman grieved for the bird. It had been a casualty of war.

Ida Saxton McKinley, 1847–1907

A TRIP TO BUFFALO AND THE FALLS

I wish we were not going a way from home.
—Ida Saxton McKinley, diary

They didn't warn her he was going to die, and small wonder, for they themselves thought otherwise. On opening him up, they'd found holes in his stomach, his pancreas, and one of his kidneys, but the bullet was lost, hidden somewhere in the muscles of his back, they supposed, and they'd left it there when they darned the wounds and closed the cut, shut him in with his septic blood, made him a cloister for moist gangrene. He'd die in seven days, but they didn't know that, and therefore little was said of his rapid pulse, his sweats and cooling off, and blithely they fed him by enema while he descanted on the grandeur of the Falls. He was dying, but the tidings all stayed good, and his wife was persuaded out of doors, taken for a drive.

She knew, though. A lifetime ill herself, she well knew when death was in the air. She had the little *mal*, and she could tell it was coming, sense it still a long way off. Her squint, her stare, the sudden cease of speech and motion— they merely made her more aware, and though nothing flew, she stood in the shade of wings. She knew. *I hope the Lord will take me with my Precious*, she wrote. *I wish we were home.*

As the carriage rolled on Main, on North, on Delaware, as spires were passed, and trees, and lawns, and many mansions, she may have wondered who'd bring her stick, take her arm, pick her up and carry her, who'd cover her face with a napkin, a doily, a bit of lace, when the wind that none could see began to touch her hair, when she grinned or twitched or glared, grew stiff, spent a moment going nowhere and a moment coming back, played the next card, ate the next bite, forgot she'd been away. *My Precious left us this morning about two o'clock*, she wrote. *I hope the dear Lord will take me very soon.* Who, she may have wondered, who would now be there?

Sarah Orne Jewett, 1849–1909

ON READING A COLLECTION OF HER LETTERS

> *Please find all that I write without ink.*
> —Sarah Orne Jewett

She wrote much and to many people, to twenty at a sitting, sometimes thirty—how she must've drained herself, how prodigal with days! She relished letters all her life, even those in books, Sainte-Beuve's, Thackeray's, Harriet Beecher

Stowe's. She wrote to family, friend, editor, to the aspirant writer, to the unknown addressed but once—she opened her hand and from it flowed. She spoke to these of books, her own and others, of the daily round, of her lifelong love for the things of Maine, she spoke of illnesses, spoke of the lost to the one forlorn, of her dog *General*, of horses and the horse that threw her, killed her, really, of the tour now being taken, the visit being planned.

To all such, all that and more, one hundred and forty-two letters in a small and scholarly volume, with notes on date and place, on her penmanship and punctuation, notes with quirk unkinked, identity supplied, a well-crafted work on the whole, quite pleasing to the eye. Strange, therefore, the lack on every page. No man is mentioned—why?

The clothes she chose were dark, and rare was the ribbon, the flash of relief, but she was comely enough, as all agreed—indeed, to some, to women, she was more: a beauty, tall, full-figured, and she seemed to sail, rather like a ship. Oh, she was one to behold, yes, and one to be held, and they rejoiced that men remained so blind. None wrote to her, or if they did, they wrote too late: her mind by then was somewhere else, and she was saying *Please find all that I write without ink.* . . .

A neighbor woman, name unknown, 1908

THE PRECIOUS STONE

The two flats were served by a fire escape common to both kitchens, and from either of these, the other could be seen, an image of itself in reverse. Along a wall of each, a gas range stood beside an icebox, face to face with a wall of cupboards across a space of floor. In the winter, heat from the stove would fog the window, and sometimes you'd erase it with your sleeve and stare through the glade at a tumble of snow in the air shaft. The flakes fell slowly in that windless well, you could almost follow them down with your eye, and they piled in wide wales on the rails of the fire escape, a mat of white corduroy spread before the flat next door. In the summer, the window was always open, and often, while your mother talked with the woman across the way, you'd climb out onto the fire escape and peer between the iron strips at the lower landings, at flowerpots, a cat on a sill, a boy with a bat and ball.

You can't recall what was spoken past you from one kitchen to another: you heard the voices, your mother's and the neighbor's, but for all you knew, there were no words, there was only a murmuring, as between two chipper birds. And yet you remember the stone, you can see and feel it still, you've never forgotten the stone! It was smooth, as though gnashed by the surf, ground among other stones, and, red in hue and nearly round, it looked not a little like a plum. You weren't told where the woman had found it or why she'd brought it home—it was simply a plum-like stone—but she thought it rare and prized it, and rare and prized it became to you. You can't say, you could never say, why that one stone was so enviable, but whenever it comes to mind, you hone, now as then, to own it, to hold it in your hand.

A day came when you did own it, a day when, unseen by your mother or the neighbor, you crawled across the fire escape, took the stone from a drawer, and bore it off to your room. There for a time you toyed with it, turned it in your fingers, palmed it, held it up to the light, tasted it, even— you owned it, you thought, the red stone plum belonged to you. And then other things drew you, a hook-and-ladder and its always galloping team, a box filled with bricks of colored clay, lead soldiers on one knee and firing, and the stone was put aside, allowed to roll away.

You must've fallen asleep on the floor—you're there, you think, when your mother awakens you, and all about you are tin and leaden presences, paper, wood, and plasticine. But it's stone that your mother softly inquires about, stone that the red stone face behind her demands without a sound. *Julian, did you take this lady's stone?* your mother says, but

71

you're looking up at the anger just beyond her, and you say nothing. *Julian*, your mother says, *did you take the stone?*, And now you bring it out from under a corner of the bed, hand it to your mother, relinquish it forever, and she gives it to the woman, saying something quietly and listening to something loud (*the little thief!* was it?), and then the woman goes away.

Mrs. Stephen Crane, 1865–1910

CORA, *MI CORAZON*

Good people love hearing about sin.
—Cora Crane

In Jacksonville, her joint was spoken of as a boarding-house, but it must've been a borderline boardinghouse, be-cause if you could buy a bed and meals there, you could also, with the wrong sort of luck, buy the clap. *Hotel de Dream*, she called the place, a sweet name for the same old stew, and it drew the inkhorn trade, among them the skinny wonder who wrote for the New York *Press*. One of his books had shown up sooner than he did, so in a way madam could claim she'd met him before. She was no reamed-out whore, though, that Cora Taylor, no emptied bag of tricks, and he found that out, and more, on the first trip he made to her room. His fall to doom was four years off and far away, but she was still with him when he fell—in the next century, it was, at Badenweiler (spa, Kurhaus, equable climate, park of fifteen acres). After that—well, where for her but Jacksonville, where else but that dream hotel?

Mary Baker Eddy, 1821–1910

FAITH IN THINGS UNSEEN

All is God, hence All is Good.
—Mary Baker Eddy

It was hard to tell whether her sentences were coming or going—they read equally well from the front and ass-end-to—but despite what she wrote about God, He wasn't quite as all-good as she claimed: the first half of her ninety-year life was an all-bad dream. Born frail, she wasn't expected to have a second half, not with those fits she had, those spells when she fell to the floor, screaming through a sponge of spit and voiding in her drawers. Sound was pain to her, or so she said, and they had to deaden the road that ran past her room, and there was something wrong with her spine (it was a cross, and she was on it! she contained her own crucifixion!), and almost as late as her wedding day, she had to be rocked to sleep in a cradle or cribbed in her father's arms. There were seizures when voices cried her name, and she required mesmerists, morphine, a hired man to keep her down—ah, she couldn't live long, poor thing, those throes would undo her, she'd swoon some day and never wake, death would come and take her off.

She was on the small side, all say, meagerly made but with a graceful way of going, and her eyes at times would change size, it seemed, and color, and she wore her hair in spirals around a rouged and powdered face. She struck poses chosen from picture books (piety, pity, disdain), and though neither bright nor pretty, she used her middling mind and looks to win three husbands and the odd and suety swain: there was always a whiff of lard about her, there was always an Ebenezer, an Asa, a Calvin flipping up her clothes. Still alive at five-and-forty, she'd grown to be a scold, drier, thinner, a chiller of desire, a slow- or no-pay boarder, a guest but seldom and snotty then, high-and-mighty with her host, a slob about the house, and purposely late for meals. A fighty

73

kind of squatter, she was, and one night, the bag and her baggage, she was kicked out in the rain.

What made her live through those dreary, deadbeat, threadbare years, unwell and unwelcome, pinched for the price of staying and the cost of going away? Why go on, when where she knocked there was no answer? Why with those fits and fears she had, that bad back of hers, that passion she suffered on a hidden cross, why did she stand there outside the door, why did she bear the pain, what did she hope to gain from a future like the present and the past? Who can say, when she herself may not have known?

That was the first half of her life, and it ended as though half was all she'd get. She'd taken a spill (the fall in Lynn, they call it now), and no knife could reach the hurt, no medicine still it, and there was no one to deaden the sound outside or hold her in his arms—she'd never walk again, it was said, never leave her bed except for a colder grave. And then in her strait, there came to her a name, *Phineas, Phineas*, and softly she uttered it, remembering a layer-on of hands in the state of Maine, *Phineas, Phineas*, and she seemed to hear him speak, saying that health was truth and sickness error, that the body was all in the mind, and the mind through faith could expel what ailed it—*Phineas, Phineas*. Mouth of brass, she knew it meant, and from it she drew another five-and-forty years of life. *Mirabile dictu*, she was healed at last!

Or so she swore—which was enough to give her a start in the paramedical art of curing the rest of the world. If she was as good as her word, she worked many marvels: she made a felon disappear, and a clubfoot unkinked when she touched it with her hand; fevers abated for her, dropsies drained, and a prolapsed uterus returned to place; the halt ran, the deaf heard, and a case of endometritis was unseated by her eye, and consumptions likewise, diphtheric throats, cancers of the breast and neck, one of the latter so far progressed that the jugular was exposed; she banned the pain of childbirth merely by her presence, and carious bone stopped stinking, and though she lost her own, she grew teeth for others, uppers, lowers, and once a whole new set of thirty-two; and while far from his pillow in Long Branch, she treated Garfield's wound by force of will until magnetic malice killed him. . . .

No more days now of making ends meet, of lacking friends, a home, a spare pair of gloves, a greeting in the street, love, a reason for sleeping and another for waking up. All her needs were filled, or all but one: the immortality she promised her followers she couldn't find herself, and saying *There is no death* to the end, she died at four score and ten. Of the three or more millions she left behind, she gave nothing to the poor: poverty, like sickness, was an error of the mind.

Three women, unnamed, 1910

TAR-PAPER SHACK

Planked down in the sagebrush, it looks rather like a box-car strayed from a right-of-way. If the renegade had wheels once, they're gone now, and there are windows where its heralds might've been, and its bituminous skin is grafted on with nails. Before it, three figures stand on worn grass, a woman and two young girls, all three in aprons newly washed and white enough to cringe the eye. There's nothing else in sight, no other people, no stock or still machines, no dogs, no dolls, no wire, no roads or wheel tracks through the weeds, only that black and smokestacked shanty, only those three in white. White flags, those aprons, but they signal no surrender; while they fly, there's no defeat.

[Photograph in a family album.]

Auld Acquaintance (P. G.), 1910

CHILDE JULIAN, BOY KING

You were six years old, and on the morrow, at your birth-day party, you'd be crowned king of the kindergarten, and you'd rule your subjects, children too, all through the long, the endless reign of a summer's afternoon. There'd be a procession in the courtyard of the school, and robes of purple paper would be worn and stoles of ermine crape, and there'd be a banquet royal of cake and ice cream, and the loyal would come with tribute and lay it at your feet—pencil boxes, tins of paints, tops, sacks of marbles, and (please!) an agate that would never miss.

Now, on the eve of your coronation, one last rite re-mained to be performed: your choosing a queen for the ever-green day. Making the choice, though, would be ceremonial only: she who'd wear your diadem was all but named, well-nigh known. She was the daughter of a neighbor who lived in the flat above your own, and whenever she came to mind, you saw her as something gray, a color in the rain, and for all you knew the rain was real, for she always seemed to you quenched. There was no good will between you, and neither was there ill: there was no will at all. Even so, with no word said, both she and her mother had managed to draw a pledge from the absence of a denial, and because it was all one to you, you let their inference lie.

When school ended for the day, the kindergarten girls were lined up and put on display, as though some seigniorage were being arranged for you, a first-night right at six!, and you were bidden to pass your vassals and single out your bride. Only one of these could win your favor—indeed, it was already won—wherefore the rest merely endured your eye and wished it would pry somewhere else. It came to you, as you moved along the line, that you were *seeing* many of the girls for the first time. You'd been in the same room with them for a year, you'd passed them in the street, spoken to them, called them by their names, even, but never until now had you gone beyond the faces, voices, shades of hair. They were separate, you saw at last, they were single and different things, and no two, like clouds, were quite the same—and all at once one of them simply reined you in. Before, she'd been part of a mass, a brick in a brick wall, a voice, a name, a forgotten shade of hair—but she was beautiful! beautiful! and you were filled with wonder, ravished, as you took her by the hand and turned to the teacher: you'd found your queen.

From further along the line, there was a lone and anguished cry, and you forgot it never. It was in your mind all night—you dreamed it—and it was still there the next day, when you were crowned king and skipped about the courtyard with your queen, the unforeseen. Of the one you hadn't chosen, you told yourself *She wasn't pretty*, but her cry was there through your day-long reign and lifelong memory. *She wasn't pretty*, you told yourself, but what you'd done, and you knew it, was make her think the same.

Jennie, in *Jennie Gerhardt* (1911)

THE WOOD DOVE

A voice of sweetness in the summer-time.
—Theodore Dreiser

Who would've thought the tone-deaf Dutchman had an ear for birds? In that immensity of words, who would've sought a sense of pitch, a response to consonance and measure, to *the rhythm of time unrolling?* His bent-wheel prose bucked and plunged him, and he seemed to fling about, flounder, lurch on the page, and surely at any phrase he'd founder and fall: he was lost, one would've sworn, to *a voice of sweetness in the summer-time*.

And yet how often in dwelling on Jennie he was mindful of the dove! It was as if he saw and heard each in the other, as if song and speech were one, and reciprocal the ways of the

77

woman and the bird. Dense proseur, graceless breaker of cadences, ill-assembled sod, still and all he was alive to their accordance, and sweet were their voices in the summer-time.

For such like creatures, it was always summer-time, a special season, like youth, that had no clear beginning and could therefore hardly end, a continuum in which nothing changed, nothing, until it all changed at once and ended in a flash. But while it lasted, it was a new element, benign and exaltative, and Jennie, as the dove did, lived in it, moved through it, soared on its sustaining airs. What a wondrous quality, that softness of nature! Plumage is all it was, but somehow it made her proof against the imminent world, a bird impervious to shot: her armor (feathers! down!) was her very lack of armor, her firmness was in her yielding. The seven ages that others underwent seemed to pass her by. They lived, and living changed them, killed them in stages, and they died. But Jennie, holding fast to nothing, was there at the last, still soft, still giving, and her voice was sweet in the summer-time.

Triangle fire victims, 1911

TWELVE DOZEN GIRLS

One of them shall not fall on the ground without
your Father.
                                        —Matthew 10: 29

Girls they were, but birds they seemed to be, perched there on the window-ledges ten stories up from the street. Below them stones, behind them flames, above them your Father making a needless sun, making one more star. And then they flew or tried to fly, those jenny wrens, those jew and dago Gibson girls, they filled the air, they turned and tumbled, streaming hair, and their plumage burned, their down of voile and bombazine, and end over end they went, those sprawling wop and sheeny girls, those flambant birds,

78

those falling lives. It was ten flights to the deadlights in the pavement, and the bodies broke them, broke the street itself when they struck it, and the fires went out, went up in smoke.

Under oath one day, there'd be those who'd say that doors were locked or hung to open inward, against the flow of panic, and they'd swear, some, to blocked aisles and cluttered floors, to dark and narrow stairs, and the Court would hear of hoses unused or useless, of drafts that forced the blaze, and depositions would be read, attestations would be made—but it would come to nothing in the end, that apodixis of guilt, and the two on trial would walk away free. The blame for the twelve dozen dead would be on the dead themselves (they'd jumped) or on God, who'd let them fall.

Twelve dozen, a gross of girls, to them as they lay in the gutter with their purses, their shocked-off shoes, their spare parts, their singed and sodden hair, to them it no longer mattered who or what had killed them: they were dead now, torn, soiled, burst open, charred. Six of them, unknown, would go unclaimed, like worthless parcels, and they'd be buried as numbers (one would be 50, one 103); the rest would reach hell or heaven with their kike and ginny names. Your Father wouldn't even know they were there. He'd be working on another firmament or possibly another fire.

Unknown woman, Triangle fire, 1911

IN EVERGREEN CEMETERY

During an all-day April rain, seven coffins were placed in a common grave, and she's in one of the six that're numbered, or she's in the seventh, which is not. If she was entire when found after the fire, she's marked 46 now, or 50, or 95; but if only a part of her was left, her head, say, her arm, her baked heart, she's in the box that contains such things, the spare feet, the thighs, the sets of toes and fingers (incomplete), and

79

she goes to Evergreen dust nameless, unnumbered, quite unknown: she ends.

And because she ends, she must've had a beginning—in the Carpathians, it might've been, or at Chiavenna, where the road comes down from the pass. There must've been those who knew the sound of her voice, the color of her hair, knew whether she was plain or pretty, quick to learn or lost. Somewhere she must've stirred for the first time, seen, heard, somewhere she must've taken the crooked mile that led to water, led to here, a certain room on a certain street. She must've begun, because on a day now twelve days old, she left that room, that street, and hastened toward this end.

She died on Washington Place, near where it crosses Greene. She was afire, her dress, her hair, her drawers, when she jumped from a window ten flights up, and she's Number 103 now, or Number 113—or, if she stayed there on that tenth floor, she burned at her machine, where the flames caught her as she was sewing sleeves of voile, collars of bombazine, and she's in the seventh box, a charred hand, perhaps, a femur, a matching pair of knees. The hair combs, the garter, the russet shoe with the buttons gone, they must have belonged to her, and the rosary, that too.

A corsetière's, 1912

A DRESS FORM NAMED. . . .

She was always there, just inside the entrance to the shop, and she seemed to be waiting for you to pass, to speak, and if you'd spoken, you liked to think, surely she would've replied. From the doorway came a sweet sigh of textiles, flowered, striped, and plain, and you breathed it deep, as if to sense it more than once. It was womanly, that fabric fragrance, like the speech of traipsing skirts—it was her bouquet, and it made your mind see through the flutes and winds of dotted swiss, the down on duvetyne, and in the night of

day you dreamed of half-rounds and the dales that lay between.

A time came when there was no array, no muslin fold, no
swathe of satin, and you saw the stand she stood on, the black
felt torso, the band of nickel, her neck: undone then the
fancy. Thereafter you looked away in going by, nor did you try
to save the savor of the zone—the dream was over, you
thought, and you'd feign no more. But why, you'd often wonder, did you wish you hadn't seen her spine, her rudimental
arms and that lattice of wire? Why was the sight a violation,
an espial? Why did you feel worn, self-abused, as if it were
your own mother you'd come upon nude? And was that why,
you'd wonder on, you never gave the form a name?

Unknown woman, Harlem, 1912

THIS EMPTY ROOM

Supper-smells swirled past you from the kitchen and into
the courtyard dusk. In the facing wall, lights were coming on,
here and there a claw of gas, blue and grasping, and here and
there a glow in glass. Clotheslines crazed the sundown glaze
on the sky, and three phone poles leaned against the evening.
Somewhere in the area, a sink began to drink, and elsewhere
something fell, and you heard a doorbell ring, a piece of china
smash, but nothing really mattered except the woman you
were watching through the gloom.

—She sat in a dimming room, waiting for a different bell
to ring, one that would bring her to her feet, attract her to a
black box affixed head-high to the plaster, a black connection
between two black worlds. As yet, though years had passed,
no such call had come.

—Wire strung the earth in staves, it lay in waves beneath
the seas, it bound the hills, lashed down towns, made snags
for kites and snares for birds, all this that at any hour of the
twenty-four, someone (in Ireland? in Labrador?) might in-

81

quire *Harlem 757?* and she across the yard say *Yes!* As yet, though years had passed, no such call had come.

—What was her name, her age, the color of her eyes and hair? What faith did she embrace or did she none? Was she afraid of heights, street crowds, constrictive places, death? What foods did she favor, were her breath and body sweet? Did she entertain and, if so, whom, boys, other women, strays brought in from the rain? Did anyone know she was alive, and would he (from hell? from heaven?) call *Harlem 757* and say *Wait, my love, I'm on the way?* As yet, though years had passed. . . .

Your mother came up behind you and put her hands on your shoulders, saying, "Why do you always stare at that window over there?"

"What window?" you said.

"The one across the yard. Is it because you think the woman is crazy?"

"I don't know."

"She really isn't. She's just lonely."

"I look and look," you said, "but I don't know why."

—In the darkness, the woman thought *I could go downstairs and call myself—but who'd hear the bell in this empty room?*

Zenobia Frome, in *Ethan Frome* (1911)

THE HEROINE

. . . she answered solemnly: *"I'm a great deal sicker than you think."*

—Edith Wharton

I'm on every page of that book. I don't mean I'm in sight from first to last, doing things, speaking, being spoken to. I mean I'm there when you can see and hear me, and I'm also there when you can't: I'm in the lines of print and in between,

82

I'm always in your mind. Ethan thinks the book's about him, and if she did any reading these days, Mattie Silver'd think it was about her, and the town of Starkfield, I suppose, would hold it to be about the two of them taken together. But it's no such thing: it's about Zeena Frome all the time, and if I'm wrong, then I'm not minding a pair of cripples, and they're free to prance away.

It's been twenty-four years since they went for a coast on that sled. Twenty-four years I've been seeing to the wants of those two, him with his crooked back and dragging leg, and her in that chair, too broke up to drag at all. It was half their lives ago that they tried to suicide, and what they got out of it was half-lives to live till they died. As for me, nobody ever took me coasting in the moonlight, let me sit in front and held me from behind, nobody ever wanted me so much that he'd sooner die with me than live without me, run a mile a minute into a tree and die! Oh God, to be thought so dear!

In the eyes of all, I was only an ailing woman, never well a day and doctoring far and wide for complaints deep down inside that no one, no medicine, ever seemed to reach. I was the kind, they thought, that dreamt up a sickness and then showed all the signs of it, agonized, took to bed, and whined. I could read their mind about me: I dosed myself too often, I used too many salves and embrocations, I made too much of drafts, they thought, night air, germs, palpitations, I was too believing about fads, like the electric battery I bought and never learned to use. And I could see this too—who was Zenobia, they were thinking, that her ailments counted? A fretful sort, a scold, they thought me, flat in the chest and qualmish, a nest of aches and shooting pains, and my throat was puckered, turkey-like, and what teeth I showed were false—a bad thirty-five, Zeena was, when she caught her Ethan, and him only twenty-eight years old. I could see it in their eyes: I had no right to prize myself so high.

As to Ethan and Mattie, it was all another story. He was lean and tall, tall even there in that part of the world, where tall was the general rule, and he gave off a feeling of power, and there was something about his face that made you think of stone statues. And Mattie Silver—well, what's there to say except she was younger even than he was, twenty, maybe, good-natured enough, a little unhandy, but kind of pretty once she got rid of that consumptive city look. It was every bit in their favor, the way Starkfield regarded them, and it was the other way round as to me. In between them two, it seemed like I was only there for my disadvantage, as if sickness was what I deserved, and they deserved to shine.

She was a pauper cousin of mine, making the family rounds, and when finally it came my turn to have her in, she and Ethan took to each other from the start. They didn't know it then, but I did, I could even see it grow. I didn't do anything about it, didn't think I had to, till the night he went to fetch her from the dance. By that time, it was so real a thing between them that I could feel it in the air, like the heat above a stove, and I made up my mind to send her away. Being she was there by sufferance, she couldn't take a stand, and anyways, she'd already stayed her stay, but Ethan struggled a little before he gave in, but give in he did. That's when I found out that for all his size and show of force, he was only a weakly man inside. I'd never known it before, but I was a long way the stronger of us, and I must've been so taken up with the thought that I didn't think any further. If he'd been up to his looks, I should've figured, he'd've put me out instead of me putting Mattie, or else he'd've gone off with her and left me in the lurch. When he didn't do either of those things, I should've known he was too weak to want to live. I didn't think, though, so I stood by my decision to send the girl away.

Then there was that downhill ride to kill themselves, ending with her in a chair and him with a crimp in his back and a short leg—and me looking after the pair. A fat lot they got out of it, but sometimes when I look at them looking at each other, I think Oh God Oh God, to be so dear, to be died for!

Martha, 1885–1914

AGONY IN ANOTHER GARDEN

The eye searches in vain; the bird is gone.
—John J. Audubon

She was a passenger pigeon, the last of multitudes, and at the age of twenty-nine, she died in desolation, the dried-up world of a cage. A pound or so in feathers, she may have been found there by some child passing by, a keeper, a seller of balloons, a finger of light from the sky, but whether she was flying when her call came or perched somewhere and preening, no one can say, for no one saw her sprawl in flight or, dying on a branch, fall to the ground dead, the last of her kind and already beginning to fade. The blue-gray head, the red-brown throat, the pound in plumage, on the way down they dimmed, and the species was now extinct.

They flew in such numbers once that the stars seemed sparse beside them, and few the grains of sand. They nightened day, they set the sun, and there was darkness on the land until they'd flown away. How did the infinite come to be bounded, how did so many shrink to one, to Martha, the last of myriads, and finally to none?

Sporting prints show fowlers firing at storms of birds, and down they pour, deluge them, and still they fire, fire, as though in birds they meant to drown—their very dogs seem doleful, they do not understand. And there are pen-and-inks of snares and traps, of nets that clap like hands, and there are half-tones of clubbing sprees with oars, bats, boards studded with nails, and there are nest burnings in diagram, and drawings explain the usages of sulphur smoke, of alcohol on grain, and there are photographs of pigeon shoots where the dead bury the sward and the dead bury the dead. Infinity therefore shrank to one, to Martha, and on a certain day, a pound and some of down, blue, gray, reddish brown, died and fell to the ground.

Would the killers, having killed all else, fall on each other and kill some more, until on a certain day they were down to one—a woman, say, a wingless mateless Martha—and alone in the garden, would she agonize or merely sit and stare, await the sound of wings?

A teacher at P.S. 81, Manhattan, 1913

MISS BLAUVELT

You were nine years old then, and you didn't know that the name was Dutch and that it meant *field of blue:* to you, it was simply the word you used when you spoke to her or evoked her with your mind. *Miss Blauvelt*, you'd say or imagine, and she'd be there and real or there behind your eyes. Nor were you aware then that you loved her, not at nine. You knew only that in her presence you had to remember to breathe and that the air seemed rinsed, as by a summer rain.

Her hair was braided and worn in a crown, and her face seemed part of her jabot, lawn, it might've been, and in a skirt that reached the floor, she appeared to be something borne, something on the wind, and you could hear her coming toward you and hear her going away; leaves, she sounded like, she made the sound of leaves.

She was your teacher for only a month, but you thought at the time that she'd always taught you and that the term would never end. She'd sail those aisles forever, skim past you on feet you couldn't see, trail the scent of sandalwood through that classroom or the fancied one in your head: there'd be no change; at nine, there was no change.

A day came when she said she had something to tell you, and you stayed after the class had gone for the day. You stood before her desk, you remember, staring at the locket she wore on a velvet ribbon, and you heard her say that she'd not be there the next morning—*lavender velvet*, you thought—no, nor any other morning: she was going to be married, she said. It was as if she'd spoken of a sickness—*going to be married,*

86

going to be dead—and the room went gray at midafternoon. You'd never see her again, you thought, and you looked up from the locket and tried to draw her in, draw her in, her face, her wreath of braids, the sound she made walking, the smell of sandalwood—you couldn't get enough!—and then you went into a dark hall that led to dark stairs. Where you were going, you thought, it was all dark.

Harriet (Chai Esther) Shapiro, 1881–1914

A DISEASE OF THE HEART

In your mother's last days, you were ten years old, and those were the days that stayed in your mind, dimming all the rest. She had a murmur, you were told, a sound made by a leaking valve, a soft, a blowing sound, it was said to be, much like that of escaping steam. It was blood escaping, but you weren't allowed to find that out, not at ten, and you thought of a murmuring heart as one that whispered, and you had to listen, you thought, or you'd miss a nearly breathless word. The word would've been death, but you never heard it, not at ten.

She tired on merely crossing a room, and her face, always pale, seemed powdered, and the beds of her nails were faintly blue, cyanotic, all such due, the doctors said, to the murmur, to a heart that spoke with bated breath. From time to time, a cough shook her, but it was shallow and single, and it hardly made her shrug. Nonetheless it was a cough, and she raised a hand as though to retrieve it, to stop it from reaching you, a small gesture, but for her all things had limitations then, all were slow, vague, scaled down, drifting.

Always you saw her briefly—you were too active, they said—but were you active, you've often wondered, because you wanted to get away? Were you troubled by her swollen wrists, her dropsical feet, by her slurred, yes, her murmured words? Did you feel she had no right to sit in that chair,

87

watching you read, play, stare at some Persian pattern on the floor? Did you think she ought to sing to you, *Rings on My Fingers*, as before? Did she make you different with her bad heart, make you unequal because she was unequal? Did she see you glance at the door, and is that what made her die?

She died that year at thirty-three, and you were free, you thought, at last....

Mrs. Abraham Nevins, 1857–1934

MOTHER OF YOUR MOTHER

The Devil shouldn't take you.
—Leah Nevins

It sounded dire—the Devil had been invoked, dread word, doom behind a domino—and with a boy of ten, it passed for a malediction. A dishonoring of elders, broken china, chairs, toys, or, worst of household sins, a mingling of vessels for milk with those for meat—for suchlike things, she'd say *The Devil shouldn't take you*, and the cast-out angel's wings would start to beat.

You were the only son of a favorite daughter, Ettie, she was called, short for Chai Esther, dead at thirty-three of— what? what kills at thirty-three? Something morbid in the heart, you were told, and in three-and-thirty years, the heart became old, slowed down, stopped. Thereafter, your own mother gone, you dwelt with hers, and though love was there, the love was strange, dark in dress, and grieving. You couldn't understand the sorrow of the aged, you didn't know that black stood for death, and death was the end: at ten, there was no end.

At ten, you were in the shade of sixty, down among the mosses and the moldering, and what you heard from above was the elegy of the gray, a lament for the fallen by those who were due to fall: the years of man were few and soon were spent. You grew in gloom you couldn't feel, couldn't fathom. No one explained your slit lapel or the crape around your arm, and the prayers you prayed in Hebrew were simply sound you made to smoothe your mother's way—to where?, when for the Jew there was no Heaven.

Wherefore the cut-glass catastrophes, the autopsies on dead and living clocks, the minglement of vessels for milk with those that were meant for meat—and *Terephah! Terephah!* your grandmother would cry, but gently, sadly, with love she'd say *The Devil shouldn't take you.* It was the only curse she knew, and it wasn't a curse at all.

Unknown woman, Washington Heights, 1915

420 CONVENT AVE., APT. D

There is a page for you in God's Book, and on that page all your deeds are written down.
—Grandma Nevins

Between Stano's Shoe Repair and Peck's, there was a grating in the sidewalk, and the billfold was lying on the grid of iron rails. Had it slipped through, it would've been at the bottom of the shaft, lost among cigar bands, buttons, matches, lead foil, the castaway of passersby. Even where it was, you nearly missed it in the winter dusk, and stooping for it, you stood for a moment in a soaring dream of riches. You realized that when you opened the billfold, the dream might change on the wing, the bird become a kite—but you had to know how much you'd found, you had to know at once! The billfold contained eleven dollars.

At first, the number seemed to limit flight, to finish off infinity. Eleven dollars, you thought, and then you spoke the words in your mind—*eleven dollars*, you said, and slowly and then suddenly the kite became a bird again, free to fly, untied. What would not those dollars buy! You walked home through a flash and color commotion of crayons, marbles, tops, jacks, balls, and tin crickets, and it was as if you were part of some great firework that was going off, a girandole, a spark fountain—eleven dollars! you thought.

When your Grandma opened the door, you displayed your find, the billfold in one hand and the cash in the other, six singles and a five, and you were so marveled by the money that you hardly knew it was the billfold your Grandma reached for. While you were staring at the silkshot banknotes—eleven! you thought—she was trying pockets for what you'd overlooked. From one of these, she drew a grayed card, and through its smirch a dim address appeared—and the dream, the bird, fell from the sky to die at your feet.

After supper, your Grandma said, she'd give you a dime, and you'd take the streetcar to the Heights and return the money, and all through the meal you were silent, thinking of the bird sprawled in death before you, feathers that would fly no more. But on your way uptown, a small hope stirred—a reward, you thought—and the bird, not yet dead, stirred too. A reward—it'd be less than eleven dollars, of course, but it might be three (feebly the bird tried to rise), and it might even be five (and the bird now feebly flew!).

Apartment D was on the third floor of Number 420, a walkup. You rang the bell, and after a while the door opened, and in a six-inch crack, a woman's face seemed to be suspended in the gloom. She said nothing; she merely peered. Showing her the billfold, you asked her if she'd lost it, and still she stood there, hung there, mute. You told her that you'd found it in Harlem (in Harlem three miles away, you said) and that you'd give it to her if she knew how much money it held. She spoke at last, saying *Elf thaler*, and because the words meant what you'd feared, you handed her the billfold, and the door closed. You waited for a time, but you knew it would stay closed. In the dark hallway, you seemed to hear a rustling—as of feathers, you thought—and something struck the floor of your mind.

New Orleans prostitute, 1915

IN THE "QUEER ZONE"

The district set aside for fast women by law.
—Storyville *Blue Book*

From outside the frame of the picture, a ramp of sunlight leads down to the room.

It brightens white and dims gloom, gleams on a brass bed, the rim of a glass, darkens corners, shadows, the far side of things it passes by. It slants across a woman just below her face, and it strikes the floor in a flow that climbs a wall to a shelf of dolls, a frieze of frozen witnesses. It touches a stand for a gramophone, glints on the crank, wets the mouth of the horn.

The woman is partly dressed and alone. She sits at a table, holding a cigarette that sends a small storm, a squall into the air, but she seems to be unaware of the smoke commotion, seems instead to be somewhere else, away from her pretty dolls smiling at nothing, away from the room, the street, the city, the *queer zone* called the world. Perhaps she is listening to a black voice coming from the throat of the gramophone, tin that some old soul is burnishing to silver, turning into gold.

And perhaps that ramp of sunlight leads upward and out of the room.

[Anonymous photograph.]

Unknown girl, Harlem, 1915

THE FALLING SICKNESS

Poor misfortunate child . . .
—someone said

Accompanied by a woman, her mother, you supposed, she was coming toward you down the avenue. You were alone, you remember, and headed uptown, but when you try to amplify the direction, to see where your excursion had begun and where it was meant to end, it seems to contract to a particular square of sidewalk, to start and finish on one particular slate: there was nothing behind you, and more of the same lay ahead.

You hardly noticed the woman—she was older and therefore old—but you were much aware of the girl, of her white shoes, white stockings, white gloves and purse. It was the white that caught your eye, the white you saw in the sun, and for some reason the glare drew you, and you stared at reflected light. Only a long time later—the next day? the next year?—did you realize how silent the street had been when the girl began to scream. It was as though the sun itself had screamed and then exploded, and all that brightness was strewn upon the ground, hat, purse, beads, and, resting on its side, one of the white suede shoes, fled from the disaster but dead all the same.

The girl had fallen, and she was lying on that ashlar, her head wrung and her eyes rolling, and held down by the woman and a bystander, her body heaved in clonic spasms, and you saw blood on her mouth, and brown and yellow stained her drawers. Someone took you by the arm and moved you away, but what you took along was a memory of whiteness marred, as though the sun were soiled.

Audrey Munson, (?)–(?)

MODEL FOR A BRONZE OF POMONA

a beautiful maiden with fruits in her bosom
                    —*Encyclopedia Britannica*

She's a myth herself now, a green and brown Pomona. Little but her name is known, another likeness in another place, perhaps, a figure on a pedestal, a face somewhere on a wall, and that is all. In some list, some liber, her date of birth may be entered and her date of death if dead, but like the garden deity, she too waits *with fruits in her bosom* for a swain to come along—Vertumnus, god of the changing year—waits for him to woo her in disguise, to win her when revealed.

Poised on a dais of water six steps up from the street, she seems to have paused in her strewing of abundance to scan the passersby. If so, she seeks no glow amid the crowd, no nimbus drawing near: she looks for Pomona's crone, a bent and grayed old woman, leaning on a stick. From her, as Pomona did, she'll hear of Anaxarete, whom the gods turned to stone on her spurned lover's tomb. And she'll be kissed by the old one in a way the old don't kiss, and she'll wait *with fruits in her bosom* for the rags and the stick to be discarded—and then she'll come down to him (for it's he, and she's Pomona!), come six steps down to the street.

[A sculpture by Karl Bitter on the Pulitzer Memorial Fountain (1916), Grand Army Plaza, New York.]

Hetty Green, 1834–1916

WITCH OF WALL STREET

*When I see a good thing going cheap, I buy a lot of it and
tuck it away.*

—Hetty Green

All her life she ran from death—and death was any
stranger she encountered in the street. There was a poisoner
in every loafer, a ripper, a doer-in, and the police were doom
in blue disguise. A bandage hid a gun, and so did bundle, so
did muff and dinner pail, every drayman was a burker, every
clerk a crank, and where a hand was in a pocket, it held a
ticking bomb. At night, she'd cower in a Bowery bed, a furnished room, a dim hotel, and she'd switch at a whim, telling
no one where she came from and none where she went. For
some reason, the deuce alone knows what, death pitied her
and let her live for eighty years, by which time she had two
hundred million in her poke, and only then did the stranger
touch her, the dreaded doer-in, and down she fell and died.

They say she went around in deep-dark clothes weath-
erworn to opalescence, and they say she tricked out in torn
veils, men's drawers, and furs gone bald, and sat on public
floors while she ate from paper bags. And the tale is told of
how she sold a chamberpot and then made a sale of the lid.
And she skimped on soap and stank, they say, and tellers at
her bank swear to the carriage she kept in the vault, the rub-
bers, the dresses, the railroad or two, and the pan she made
mush in on the cashier's stove. It goes the rounds that she
trussed her own hernia sooner than fee a surgeon, and that
she vetted others too, her son for one, the time he broke his
knee. She wrapped it in tobacco leaves, the story has it, and
she baked it in hot sand, and she rubbed it with oil of squills,
whatever that might've been, but the leg turned greener than
the rest of Mr. Green, and he lost it, along with half a thigh.
Schemers were after her money, she thought, and she sued
without mercy and was sued without end, and it's said that

94

she never learned to spell, never forgot a loss, never forgave a slight, and she'd sort out rags, they say, and get a penny a pound more for the white. . . .

Yet who were they that looked down their noses? Were they beau ideals, those that sneezed at her, were they gems, salt, faultless fellows all? Or were they one with the one they blackened, were they black themselves, tradesmen, scrapers of flint, flagrant in their crime of trying to grow a dollar from every God damn dime?

Sister Ruth, 1908–

AND BROTHER JULIAN

Christmas, 1916

The holiday meant nothing to either of you. It belonged to *others*, you'd been told, and therefore once each year you watched what *others* did, saw through wreathed windows their sweet and solemn joys. In the street, little evergreen forests made you breathe deep on your way to school, and displayed in many stores were the toys that would go to *others*, the boys and girls called *others*, and except for that one year, none of them was yours. . . .

That year, your uncle Dave sent you a letter from faraway Peru, and along with the letter came a ten-dollar bill, half of it for your sister Ruth, he wrote, and half of it for you. He directed that the money be spent on Christmas presents, one for her and one for yourself, and being the elder, you were to choose them both. You were to use care and good judgment, he said, and for once, as though you were *others*, there'd be presents for the Jews!

Not far from where you lived, no further in fact than the corner, there was a shop called Peck's, where candy could be bought, and school supplies, and pipes, and snuff, and ciga-

95

rettes, but in season its shelves and showcases were dense with playthings, and you'd wander among them in wonder, awed by a Flexible Flyer, agape at a set of trains. Never before, though, had you stared at such as a buyer, one who might pause, point, and cause title to pass, but now, with a yellowback in your hand, you were a customer! and you equaled the seller at last.

On entering the store, you went straight to the counter that held a magic lantern. You stood before it, fingering the red enamel on the chimney, the slide-holder, the tube containing the prism and the lens, and you could see, even then, even there, pictures glowing on a plaster wall, balsa boats on Lake Titicaca, Mount Illimani, and a chimba-chaca, as your uncle called it, a rope bridge over a gorge. A magic lantern, you thought, but it was the magic, only the magic, that the five dollars bought.

Now came your sister's turn—five dollars' worth for your sister Ruth—and what you knew she wanted, what long she'd longed for, lay ineluctable near the stereopticon: a doll house. With its front lowered and its furniture exposed, beds the size of dominoes, peewee chairs and sofas, minim chiffoniers, it sought you out and mutely dunned your eyes. You remembered how your sister had yearned through the doorway, drawn at the toy as the toy drew at you, and you knew, *knew*, how raptured she'd be when, as though you were uncle Dave, you brought it home to her, not from a shop at the corner but from faraway Peru.

You were about to buy it when what light there was in the store seemed to converge on one particular object, and in a surround of gloom, it grew luminous, as from some quantum within. You peered into the candescence, and at its core you found what caused it, a sun, a burning mass, a brass and blazing motorboat, and to you it was the prime wonder of the pastime world. Gone your memory of a sister's hunger for a small-scale house and its scaled-down things, gone all thought of her foreknown bliss. Entranced yourself, you bought the boat for your sister Ruth . . . !

Christmas, 1976

Sixty times since then, Bethlehem has toured the sun, sixty rounds the radiant manger, and still you can hear the way your sister cried, still see her face change as fancy shrank and hope died—sixty years, and still when you think of her shrunken face, you shrink too. She got the doll house, of course—your father was there, and he simply stared you and the boat out of the flat and back to the store—but it made no difference. You hadn't known what the day was for. It belonged to *others*, just as you'd been told.

Unknown woman, Long Branch, 1917

A SUMMER BY THE SEA

Each morning, you'd hurry down to the shore, and if the square white flag was flying above Reynolds' pavilion, you knew there'd be swimming that day, and soon, soon, she'd be there, lying on the beach in the sun. Soon, soon, you'd think, but unable to await her real arrival, you'd fetch her with your mind, place her just so, not too close and not too far away, shut her eyes against the glare, and watch her, unaware, subrogate the sand, mold it, smooth it, pass it through her hand. At times, though, your mind would fail to hold her, and she'd wander off along the tidemark of the night before, where dried shells lay, and weed, and from there she'd stare out at a dory headed for the nets, at a liner towed by its smoke, dragged by its hair, or at nothing more than motion.

The dream, as a rule, grew tangible at noon, and as the hour neared, you'd find yourself preparing for one particular presence, watching the staircase for one particular costume. There'd be other such and much alike, a blouse and skirt of black cotton, some faded ashen and some still asheen, but you'd see none of them, as if none of them was there—and then suddenly she'd appear on the steps, the incarnation, actuality in black. She'd cross the beach and kneel somewhere, at first she'd always kneel, in prayer it seemed save for her self-embrace, as though her arms were those of someone else, and in the end she'd lie extended on the sand.

You'd gaze and gaze at her, you'd try to make an invasion with your eyes. There'd be no black cotton bathing-dress, faded to gray or otherwise, there'd be nothing on her body but the sun, nothing to censor sight—and yet at thirteen, though you gazed and gazed, you'd see no more than you had in your mind. It did no good to suppose her clothes away: all summer long, when the white flag flew, you'd wait for her, watch her, will her to be naked, and still be blind.

The days went, and the weeks, and the summer was almost gone the morning all that trash was stranded by the tide, fruit, labels, hundreds of labels, an oar, a canteen, a Navy life-jacket, and, over near a jetty, something covered by two towels stamped *reynolds-reynolds*. You saw waves run up and touch it, as in a game of tag, and then turn and run away, and you saw people standing there as if expecting the thing to rise and run too. But not the one you were concerned with: she was looking out to sea, beyond the ropes, beyond the nets, you thought, beyond anything in sight. She reached down for a handful of sand, and still looking off, she let it pour back to the beach. The summer was over.

Unknown woman, United States, 1921

WIFE OF THE UNKNOWN SOLDIER

. . . raised in Brooklyn, in Memphis, near the lakefront in Cleveland, Ohio. . . .
—John Dos Passos, *"The Body of an American,"* 1932

Did she too come from one of those burgs, or did she hail from somewhere else, a place harder to find, harder to say, a long way off from a train? Did her house have a street and number or a mailbox standing on a welded chain, or wasn't it

known in the districk, couldn't it be reached on the phone?
In what state did she first see the light, or was it dark from
coast to coast, was night the sight she saw

in Chi, on Beacon Hill, on Telegraph . . . ?

What was her family name, was it native, like yours and
mine, something you could holler, something concise and
everyday, was it (if you get my drift) christian, nice? Was she
pretty as a child, were her fingers limber, her feet small, was
her hair worn long, and was she plain when they met, her
pretty all gone, and where did they meet, the twain,

*in Portland, the city of Roses, in Stuyvesant Square, on
the beach at Coronado . . . ?*

Did she change back to pretty while they made the
beast, did she stay that way when spent, or did he pay her no
attention, did he quickly come and quickly go to sleep? What
did she say to the things he said, and what were they to her,
those things he chose to talk of, what did they mean, reveal,
explain, what kind of mind did she have, what was the quality
of her brain, did she learn from him or teach, she who'd lain
in the sun that day

on Coronado Beach?

And what did she think when he went away to Dix,
Bragg, Benning, Devens, what when he sailed for France?
What did he write from where he was sent, and what did she
say in reply? On what day did he die, was he no longer alive
when his last letter arrived

in Memphis, in Chi, on Telegraph Hill . . . ?

Ella Downey, in *All God's Chillun Got Wings* (1924)

THE WIFE OF NIGGER JIM

Ella: I wish I was black like you.
                                   —Eugene O'Neill

That's what you heard from the stage, but it wasn't Ella talking or even Ella that you saw: it was someone I stood behind, speaking in my name but never speaking my mind. It was she out there where those three streets crossed—it was she, and, lost in her shade, I went by unseen. *I wish I was black like you*, she said, and you were made to suppose she was crazed—the fits she had, the way she swore and raged, the wildness worn at will, like clothes, such were her signs of far-gone reason. She's touched, you thought, and you didn't know she wasn't Ella.

I'm Ella, let *me* tell of Ella! I wasn't much at eight, poor, slight, small, and all I had to grow on was my color, which was white. I was old at seventeen, bolder, used, my cherry gone in some stairwell or long since left on a roof. At twenty-two, I'd had a bastard and buried it, dead of the clap or a quinsy, and I was tired all the time, pale, and my eyes were deep in my head, almost hidden, like animals peering from a cave. But if I stare at things and rarely see them, if I hear these days and don't quite follow, never think I'm not all there— I'm as right in the head as you and just as white as I was before I married Nigger Jim, whiter, maybe, because now I own a nigger slave.

He wears my ring in the septum of his nose—you can see it if you look—and he does as I wish and goes where he's told. I let him think he's a man at times, I let him plan, read, study all night—a member of the Bar, he wants to be, as if being a lawyer will fade him to white. The Bar, the Bar, he dwells on the Bar! For him, there's a spell in the word, and if he ever passes, if he's ever sworn in, Nigger Jim will be my equal, Nigger Jim will turn white. The day that happens, I'll kill him. He's black, and he gives me the right, the excuse to look down.

100

Mrs. Virgil Adams, in *Alice Adams* (1921)

MY DEAR, BEAUTIFUL GIRL

You've got a fine way to cure a sick man.
—Booth Tarkington

She doesn't seem to have had a first name. Once or twice and long ago, her husband had called her *Darling* and invoked her loving face, but he called her nothing when he spoke to her now, for she was dear to him no more, nor was she beautiful. She was simply a spatial magnitude, a solid, something that made a shadow, and remarkable only in this, that the shadow stayed behind when she'd gone.

How had she so descended, his once dear, his darling? When had that sun, that star, begun to set? What had she done or not done, said or suppressed, felt or failed to feel? Had she made small of him early (small of little?)? How near their bright morning (my dear! my dear!) did their night start to fall?

He was sick now. He'd had a stroke, and they'd brought him home from his place of work, *that hole*, as his wife had always put it, *that hole*, as though, like a mule in a mine, he earned his keep below the ground. He'd been down there for twenty-five years, draying in some blind gallery, dragging weight in some dark drift, and here he was with a stroke, a broken-open mind. *That hole*, she thought, and she flogged the beast for flagging, failing her, feeling no love for the lash. *That hole*, she thought, and she flayed him the more, made him rise again, drove him as fast as before, faster, for the time for taking time was past, and the second stroke was coming (didn't she know? didn't she care?), and then the third and last.

My dear, beautiful girl, he'd called her once.

101

Maimie Pinzer, 1885–1922(?)

MY DEAR MRS. HOWE

I have thought of you often since I was in the hospital
and have wanted to write, but some inexpressible feeling
has prevented the writing thus far. . . .
—M. P., first letter, 1910

After thirty-one operations on and around her eye, they
lost it for her, the corn-doctors!, ball, lashes, lid, and all, and
in suturing the hole, they drew her cheek up and her brow
down, and to cover the skew they'd made with their graceless
blunders, she wore a patch across her face, pink, to match her
shade of skin—a joke, because it never failed, so to speak, to
catch the eye. No one ever named her ailment, or no one
heard the word if used, but at a guess it was the syph that ate
her sight away, a retinal sore she must've picked up in the
trade: she'd been a whore from adolescence, from earlier,
even, if you counted her uncle,

Who did me the first wrong, when I was a tiny girl, and
any number of times since then. . . .
—seventy-fifth letter, 1913

At the age of thirteen, she was sworn into a school for
wayward girls on the complaint of her mother—and of her
uncle too, that selfsame uncle—but she soon ran off with a
lover named Sloan, lived with him as man and wife while
working as an actress and posing in the nude, and wound up
in a ward with the dose that crocked her eye. Lover Sloan left
her, of course, but she found herself a real-enough husband,
a carpenter with (it's true, it's true) a blind side of his own. He
made three dollars a week, in a good week four, which, God
knows how, she had to eke out with that semiprivate body of
hers, and God knows too to whom she hired it, the cigar-store
bum, the friend of a friend, the cheap-jack, God knows what
tricks she used with her sad pink patch and her one good eye.
In five years' time, she was back in some hospital, a user now
of M——, her way of putting an addiction to morphine.

While breaking the habit, she had her first word from Fanny Howe of Brimmer Street in Boston, of Cotuit on the Cape.

> *You make me feel important. . . .*
> —twenty-fourth letter, 1911

In all, Maimie wrote to her friend (they were quickly friends) about once a month for not quite a dozen years, and her letters were read and always replied to, and if sometimes shown to a second self, they were never thrown away, wherefore they exist, those 140-odd screeds, they're on deposit, and from some atheneum, they speak still, telling of human needs and of how hard they are to fill.

> *There is much misery in the world. Mr. Arons told me he hasn't tasted chicken since January 1910!*
> —fifty-first letter, 1912

She was sorry for Mr. Arons, a broken-down cigar maker with a sick wife and a hunchback daughter, and she saw to it that chicken came his way once more. Jesus, Jesus, where was Your Father's sense of shame, to let a one-eyed whore feed the failing household of a gimpy Jew! What was His reason, Jesus, why were certain lives—yours, hers, the Aronses'—made stations of the Cross?

> *I'm afraid I bore you with this perpetual talk about my small affairs—but you see, it is all of my small life. . . .*
> —fifty-fourth letter, 1912

She was wrong about that: it wasn't small at all. It merely seemed to be, what with her mother's hatred of her *nafka*, her Jewish prostitute, her brother's contumely, the homelessness of homes for a month, a week, and sometimes overnight, the pinching of every penny to make them serve as dimes. My small life, she called it, but it was many lives in one, and each of them was great.

> *I wouldn't be so kind to you if I was happy and the positions were reversed—I'd spend all my time enjoying my happiness. . . .*
> —twenty-fifth letter, 1911

103

And she was wrong about that, because what she did for the Aronses, she did for others too: no one ever knew her without tasting chicken. Hear tell of Stella Phillips, *a beautiful red-haired girl that I am trying to keep out of the gutter*. She didn't, though, and when Stella turned up with a chancre, acute gon, and TB, she fed her, bathed her, massaged her (with spikenard, was it?), and let her share her bed.

> *Somehow Stella is Maimie. Do you get the idea . . . ?*
> —ninety-eighth letter, 1915

Yes, you get the idea: she was trying to pack God's intermissions, do what He'd left undone. *There is much misery in the world*, she'd written, and she knew it all, the sickness, the handouts of small change, the scorn and odium, the name she had to wear—whore!—the exhortation of betters, the good eye, bloodshot, sore, burning as she wrote 140 letters to her one and only friend. Brave and beautiful, that Maimie was, more so than her beloved Stella, more, even, than Bethany Mary—she healed the sores of sinners like herself, which made her as brave as the Savior was, and beautiful.

> *I want to go to school. I want to take up the study of something. I know what I have yet to know*
> —last letter, 1922

And signing herself *Maimie*, she was never again heard from. She may have died, or she may have decided to write no more (she'd said once *It would be better if I dropped out of sight*) and simply lost herself in the world. But God forfend that God should lose her too: He might have a God of His own, He might have to pay some day. . . .

Fanny Quincy Howe, 1870–1933

LETTERS TO A SCARLET WOMAN

There is no inquisition in the grave.

—F. Q. H.

It's missing, all her written matter from Boston, lost, and
now none can say how her salutations ran—were they distant
in tone? *Dear Maimie Pinzer*, is that the way they began?
From round the Common and Cotuit on the Sound, those
scores of scented pages, all numbered and some of them em-
bossed, a whore's hoard, they're gone, and she's gone with
them, she too lost. They went where she did, to those fitted-
up rooms, those flats she flitted through, those thirty-watt
hotels above saloons, and if she's dead (alive, she'd be ninety),
they're with her in a swamp, a pit, a potter's field—but where
she is, there the letters are. She could never have thrown
them away.

During their twelve-year correspondence, they met but
twice, the lady and the jade, but why did they meet at all,
what drew the bluestocking to the wry-sighted Jew, what
made her heart condense, whence the pen she found in her
hand? Maimies were never seen on Brimmer Street; they
were read about, as Moll, perhaps, or Karenina, but they
were quite unknown to Commonwealth, they were foreign
to the Hill. How, then, was a Philadelphia kike, a user of
M——, a half-blind syphilitic, reached from so far away?

Dear friend, those letters must've said, and Maimie
must've read the words as spelled and meant, she must've
been impressed by the stranger who sat by her bed, quiet,
Christian, plainly dressed, she must've believed her come
there on some effusion of the spirit, an imperative with wings.
She must've been made to feel proper again—she wasn't
catching, she must've been given to understand, the lady
wasn't afraid of taint on the letters she read, on the hand she
held in her hand. In her presence, Maimie must've healed,
and in time (who knows?), she might've undone the doing of

the spirochete, grown a second eye and seen—*Y'hay sh'may
ra-boh m'vo-rach!* May His great name be blessed!

Yes, there must've been something about the lady that
was matched in the whore. In all those furnished rooms,
those one-flight-up hotels, she never quite sold her favors,
nay, she gave herself away. And the lady's life too had its stations of the Cross—how else could she have come to know of
Maimie, what else could she have written than *My very dear
friend* . . . ?

Auld Acquaintance (D. U. S.), 1924

WOOLWORTH BUILDING, 28TH FLOOR

Would it make any difference. . . ?
All the difference in the world!

You saw her for the first time on enrollment day at Ford-
ham Law School. She was at the end of a line of students
leading to the door of the bursar's office, and joining it just
behind her, you stood there waiting, and while you waited
you found yourself gazing at her hair. In the dim hallway, it
seemed to be blond, but when she moved her head, what
light it caught ran red and gold, and you thought of electric
arcs and then of nothing, and the idle moment ended. You
remembered none of it until another moment came, and you
knew then that you'd remembered all. In one of the courses
you were taking, the two of you were seated in the same row,
and the sun, low down over the Hudson, hit the building with
level rays, lit the classroom, lit her hair, and again it glowed
with plays of red and gold.

You spoke to her for the first time that evening—what
did you say, and what did she?—and then you were walking
with her in the downtown dark, across the park and toward
the Bridge—what did you say, and what did she?—and somewhere, near someone's statue, was it?, was it Nathan Hale's?,

you stopped to look back and upward at the dime-store cathedral.

Would it make any difference, you said, *if I told you I was a Jew?*

And staring as at an intruder, she said *All the difference in the world!*

Her middle name, you learned later, was Ursula, for the saint slain by the Huns along with her train of eleven thousand virgins. That was in the third century.

All the difference, and she never spoke to you again.

Mrs. Jack Gardner, 1840–1924

SELF-ABASEMENT ON BRIMMER ST.

Mrs. Jack Gardner is the most vigorous observer of Lent among society leaders. She wears black serge garments fashioned after the manner of a sisterhood, with a double row of black beads at the waist, and she drives several times a day in her elegantly appointed carriage, with subdued Lenten liveries, to the Church of the Advent. . . .
—a Boston paper

The Day of Ashes had passed, and the days of fast were here, fewer than forty now, for the Resurrection was drawing near. She'd made her prayers in the proper places and properly in serge, she'd put the world behind her, worn her dust reminder—*memento, quia pulvis*—until it wore away, but for all her lustration, sin seemed still within her, and sinner she remained. By now, she'd had her warning, angina the year before in Seville, and rising fifty, she may have dwelt on flying time and dying out of grace, on her heart's end and the start of her damnation. When, therefore, *in her elegantly appointed carriage*, she came one day to her Back Bay church, no lectionary was seen on her black serge lap, no Book of Common Prayer. Instead, a bucket of sudded water, and with this, on her black serge knees, she washed the steps of Ad-

107

vent's stoop. In their *subdued Lenten liveries*, two footmen and a coachman watched.

Straight to Beacon spread the word, and there it split to spread both ways, and laughter was heard in Brookline and heard as well up the Hill. On her shins in Brimmer Street— she who'd bathed in the Dead Sea, drunk from the Jordan, she who'd been robbed in Bethel! How droll, the role of penitent, how odd, the kind of God she hoped to find with soap! It was too rare, really, to relish in private, and scarcely dressed for calling, they called all the same. The laughter grew: some hadn't stopped for stays.

But why the high old time? What was Mrs. Jack in black serge doing that none could understand? In purging those steps, she purged herself, or, if she merely thought so, was not the thought enough? But all they could see were the pearls she bought by the gross on her pilgrimage to Bethany, and of course they laughed some more.

California, in *Roan Stallion* (1924)

THE STALLION'S WIFE

She loved, she was not afraid of the hooves.
—Robinson Jeffers

It was her father who gave her the name, but being unread in the old romances, he never knew whence it came, and therefore he was dead to having called her after an imaginary isle lying offshore from Paradise—California, he said she'd be, and she was, Spic and Indian on her mother's side and begotten by a Scot. And now, rising twenty, she was married herself, to Johnny the Hollander, swiller and whoresman and sire of the child Christine, blue-eyed, one reads, but wizened, heiress of all his lowlife deeds.

Christmas was hardly a day away when Johnny drove home drunk leading Maskerel's mincing roan, won by him at

108

gaming, but gone from his head the gifts he'd promised Christine—*By God, forgot,* he said. When morning came, the woman, who could almost see the wrinkled face wrinkle more, the woman herself drove to Monterey for the picture book, the doll, the painted wooden toys, but on the way back, the mare began to tire. The fords fretted her, and at one of them she became afraid, Malpaso Creek, it may have been, or Bixby, God knows because the prose doesn't say, but it took the whip to make her try, and when she floundered and refused, California began to pray.

She prayed to gentle Jesus, dear baby Jesus, prayed in the dark for light to see the way—and there in the spate out of Palo Colorado (is that where it was?), there at the meet of salt sea and sweet water, there a miracle! Radiance, along with Latin singing—and the black deep stream was crossed with the sodden promised presents for Christine. On reaching home, the woman dried them and laid them by, and on some shelf they may have seemed to glow, another wonder.

Unthinking, she told Christine of the christian birth of long ago, of Mary the mother, of the stallion father—the what? Good God, it was God she'd meant to say! But from then on, she was a lost one, and when Johnny left for a night of whoring, she went straight to where the roan patrolled his fence, rode him, made him ride her—*unendurable violation!* And then Johnny was home again bringing wine, and he said that after he'd had a glass (fatuous Dutchman!) he'd show her *what the red fellow did.* But while he poured, she slipped away, decoyed him, and half-drunk he followed her to the red fellow's pale, and, his drunk half running him, he entered the kingdom of God, and there God killed him. Whereupon (why?) the woman went back for a gun and fired three times before God fell and died beside Johnny. . . .

All this in those seventeen pages, this and more in infantry prose, in the tread of leaden foot-soldier feet. Ah, California!

Mary Litogot Ford, 1839–76

SPEAKING OF NEATNESS, HE SAID

I get that from my Dutch mother.
                                        —Henry Ford

He was sixty at the time, and his mind was slightly roiled, like wine disturbed, and he no longer knew what he'd gotten from his mother, whether it was much or little, nor could he say for sure that her blood was Dutch. She'd died when he was thirteen, leaving behind a single likeness, and ever after he tried to stare life back into the indefinite face and features, the seemingly solid hair. Never, though, could he make them stir, those masses of black and white and gray, and they remained what they'd been at the beginning, images caught in sensitive salts.

Even so, he chose to say such things as *I have tried to live my life as my mother would have wished* (Flemish? Belgian? Dutch?), and, who knows?, maybe he wrought her will, brought on the death of the world. In her brief stay, she may have said the sesame word to him, read him the fecundative lesson from *Gems of Life*, with some spell she cast, some Low Country adage, she may have made known her aim, may have shown the way. That craze he had to make machines (and machines that would make machines!), what was it but a matroclinic lust to spawn that must've come from her?

She lies in a cemetery on Joy Road, near the town of Dearborn and nearer the River Rouge, and from there, when wind and air are right, she may hear tire treads and engines firing, she may smell the smoke of burning lives, and once in a while, with the residue of her face, she may even form a smile.

110

Isadora Duncan, 1877–1927

DIE ERSTE BARFUSS TANZERIN

I have only danced my life.
—Isadora Duncan

She didn't dance all of it with music, and she didn't always dance it on the stage. In the beds of rustic inns, *barfuss* she danced and bare-ass too, in *cabinets particuliers*, in empty rooms, in *wagons-lits* and *ateliers*, there as well, and on her back while drifting past Khartoum. She danced for Pim and his eighteen trunks of clothes, for someone she called The Ugly Pianist, for teutonic pedants, gallic pederasts, and the Duke of S. at Lake Leman, and she danced for Halle the Chelsea *délicat* and for the burning man of medicine at the *plage*, and she danced, as the years sped by and favor fled her, for companions of the hour, fellow-passengers, pickups, a few who happened to rap on her door, and toward the end, fat, drunk, all jazzed out, and broke, she danced for heavy women and a bevy of two-way boys.

Her art, she claimed, took its rise in the soul, an organ or attribute sited in her abdomen in front of the aorta and the crura of the diaphragm: it was from there, she said, and not from the head or heart, that the body's motion welled and ran. Long had she sought that font, long through days and lonely nights, still hours passed with her hands held so, crossed upon her brisket, and at last something stirred in the coeliac axis at the root of the mesenteric artery, some force began to vibrate, some *geist* began to yearn—and she danced.

Her art, she harped on, but there's nothing left of that, not even a reel of film, grained as if shot in the rain, over- or underexposed, and cranked at several speeds—nothing that moves after forty-nine years of motion that stemmed from the soul. And she dwelt on her body, that *lovely youthful naiad form*, those *lithe hands and nimble feet*, the *skin of satin*, and of such things only stills remain in the minds of bohunk Hamlets, titled triflers, and L., a maker of sewing-machines. She

111

came and went, the *barfuss Tanzerin*, she danced her life, spent it, blew it in, threw it at the wind.

In Nice, a car-wheel caught and reeled her shawl, and by the time they cut her loose, she was dead, but she'd died here and there before, and her naiad body, not now young, would flow no springs. Her breasts, hard and small once, hung like pockets turned inside-out, her feet were veined and splayed, and her sodden soul exuded beer. As for the art that was stilled when she strangled, it too had been killed by the inch, and pieces lay on many floors, on sand and sheets, on grass and the roads of Greece, on the cindered seats of third-class trains. Already gone, Isadora, when death came for her—but all the same, in that ill-written book of hers, in that vain and silly screed, she seems to unfurl and flutter yet. Language streams back from her, a scarf of words, fringed and rippling, red, even, like the real one, gay, cosmetic, free, and none need cry *Isadora! Ton châle! Ton châle!*, for no spokes will ever twist it tight and choke her, not till the book becomes dust and dances away.

Her art was her forty-nine years, and she got nearly all of it into print—her sins and innocence, her gall and greenness, her pride and her lack of pride, her easy-come and easier-go, and her vainglory (the horses unhitched by votaries! the coaches they drew through the streets!), and there are lovers on facing pages, The Archangel, one was, and another Craig, and there were shy voyeurs in the moonlight and a fongoo as bold as an Alp, and she names her footnote geniuses (who is Beaunier? who in hell Carrière?), and that pilgrimage of clowns is there, the Duncans gone to Hellas—see the staves they carry, the tunics they wear, the fillets that bind their hair . . . !

Foolish, the book, foolish, sad, appealing, rending, really, and pulsing with disarray, like the life it keeps alive.

Mrs. Nicola (Rosina) Sacco ?–?

AUGUST, 1927

I remember a years go on our love day . . .
—Nicola Sacco

She too remembered as she sleepwalked, lost, through the streets of Boston. People passed as in some chiffon dream, adrift, they came to seem, blown along and billowing, flown, almost, and there were times when she wondered whether she had invented herself as well as the world she wended, gray, cold, winter-far from the summer sun, and it was only the impounded sound of her flowing blood that told her she was real:

the dear remembrance is still rimane in my heart . . .

Lombardy, north of the Po, was her place of birth, and she had brought away from it the vividry of its women, the red hair, the white face, the space-black eyes. It was said of her, and she but thirty!, that she had been a beauty once, bright, variable, sinuous, a small and falling stream, and they say that when Sacco first saw her (*Rosina how nise she was look*), he loved her, loved her, but all that was long ago, before he was taken from her to be killed, and she was beautiful no more:

the sufferance had make her look like a old woman . . .

There were days when she walked all the way to the prison, walked, his Rosina, his Rose, as he sometimes called her, or Rosa, or Rosie, or Rosetta, dark-dressed and worn, old so young, but always, under the sufferance, he could see the transpadane luster of the Lombard plain. In a little while, always would end, and as he gazed at her through a screen of wire, he knew that she would be the last presence in his mind, not with graphed and graven face, with red hair gone dead and statuary eyes; he'd see her as she was when *we both of us went in city town, and we went in a big stor, and she was all dress up . . .*

And there were days when she walked back through the

113

crooked streets of Boston, and she heard words being spoken, music from an open window, laughter, and dogs and children broke and ran, and she saw lives lived as though they'd last forever, and as she and people passed, she thought of Nick, about to die, and she remembered:

those day . . . they was a some happy day. . . .

Auld Acquaintance (L. G.), 1927

THE HAND-ME-DOWN

She'd be good for you.

He looked in on you one night—he was passing by, he said—and she was with him, his girl, you thought, and brought for showing off. You didn't know why your favor mattered to him: you were something less than friends, and in his company, you often felt a rankle, as though a sore spot were forming for a pimple two days hence. It was strange, that sense of festering, it was hard to ascribe to his use of certain words: he said *title* when referring to a book. *I bought a title by Nietzsche*, he'd say . . . but how could such a frailty generate pus?

The girl was pretty. She wore a dark and simple dress, with little cling or conformation, but it gave you inklings all the same of unobtrusive rounds. Speaking seldom, she listened while her consort talked (of *titles*, was it?), and at times, though watching one of them, you dwelt on the other (*Why did he bring her?*, you wondered, and *How could she have come?*), but soon you were watching only her. You liked her hands, you discovered—they were decoration—and she kept them still as she heard tell of *Übermensch*, heard of *Zarathustra*. She was pretty, you thought.

He sought you out the next day to learn your opinion, and when you conveyed it, he astounded you by saying *She'd be good for you*, and then, giving you a card on which a name

114

and number were written, he walked away. You stared at the card, but what you saw was a dark dress, not quite filled, and hands like ornaments: he'd given you the girl herself, not a name and number. *She'd be good for you,* he'd said, but how could he have known?

You never let her know that he was right. You kept a smoke of words on the air, and through it notions drifted, floundered, and there were vague posturings and involutions—leaves seemed to be burning, and no wind came to clear the mind, to blow the pall away. How many miles did you walk her through that blue-gray haze, how many words were consumed that you might stay begloomed, and why, when the walks and words had ended, did you say the gloom was hers? what was it that made you lie? *She'd be good for you,* he'd said, and she would've been, but you were afraid, and you refused her. She never knew that. How could she have known . . . ?

Ina Coolbrith, 1841–1928

POET LAUREATE OF CALIFORNIA

> *I cannot sit in the shadow*
> *Forever, and sing of the sun.*
> > —Ina Coolbrith, "Marah," in
> > *Songs from the Golden Gate*

This dainty writer, Bierce called her, and he called her work *a pleasant rill of song,* and if right in what he said, he was wrong in saying it, unkind, spiteful, even for one with his feline mouth, his pouncing mind. She didn't require to be told that her light was small, rather like a firefly's, hardly light at all: she knew it, and it must've galled her life. To glint in flight and fade on the page, to be firefly no more, but a beetle on the ground—how hard to bear, the change from thought aloft to thought as written down! In a lyric on the mariposa lily (*winged bloom! blossom-butterfly!*), she addressed it as *a*

115

flower of the fields of the air, and the metaphor quivers yet, an arrow in the gold. But that was the odd occasion—the dainty writer hardly ever scored a nine.

Born Josephine Smith, she was the niece and namesake of the Mormon martyr killed in Illinois, but the pleasant little rill never ran red, it was never dyed by her dead uncle, nor did her lines dwell on her wagon-ride west, on seeing El Dorado first from Beckwourth Summit with Jim himself at her side. She simply didn't write of such things, nor of these, the husband who shouted *Whore!* at her, or the man who shot him for it. With her, it was as if events, like people, passed away, and flowers, only flowers, were perennial.

Lyricus, of or pertaining to the lyre or harp: songs are what she sang, little rhapsodies of the poppy and the rose, of skies dark with lark and linnet, of pasture, cloud, the wind, of rills within a rill of rhymes. Rare, rare the phrase wherein one sees a tree, a hill, the dew, as never seen before, the sky another blue, another green the sea.

At thirty-three—she was beautiful then, they say—she became a librarian to pay her own way, and for eighteen years, she ruled her house of books, and in the end, when it began to cant with their weight, became a leaning tower of learning, she was sent away for calling the place unsafe. Those who wrote of her say she was still beautiful at fifty—and how many there were who mentioned her! how many loved her! They found other work for her that yielded other honoraria, and when the Fire burned her out except for what she wore, they concerned themselves and bore a part of her loss.

She was aging now, the dainty writer, and she *listened back*, as she put it, but only to roses gone from her window, to no longer falling rain, to snow and silence. And in that snow and silence, for all the honors she'd won—Laureate!— all the praise, how hard it must've been to know that Bierce had bestowed the only bays and laurels she had earned! how heavy the wait for the grave!

116

Lady Brett Ashley, in *The Sun Also Rises* (1926)

THE CHRIST-KILLER

That kike!
                              —Bill Gorton
Take that sad Jewish face away.
                              —Mike Campbell
I hate him. I hate his suffering.
                              —Brett Ashley

I did not hate Robert Cohn; none of us hated him. None of the chaps, Jake, Bill, Mike, nobody hated him but Ernest, and it was Ernest who made us say those things; we would never have said them on our own. But it being his book, and we being there by the grace of Ernest, we belonged to him, and we did as we were told. Therefore, when he said bait the Jew, we baited, and when he said hate, we hated with the best—but that was not what any of us would have done if Ernest had let us be.

You can have a good life, being a character in a book. If you are truly written, as Ernest says somewhere, and if, as he says somewhere else, you have the courage to work in close, thus making a pure line with the bull, then you cannot really die. You will live on in those pages, doing forever what assuredly would end some day if you were only flesh and blood. If you are well and truly made, it is a good thing to be a thing of words; the horns will never touch you, and you will never die.

In a book of Ernest's, most of the time you will be with people who make you feel good. They will do and say the things they should, giving no offense that they know of and throwing no pride away, and so when you are in their company, you will come to feel that in all the world there is no better place to be. You will drink champagne from tumblers with such people, you will eat without end, and how fine the music and the dancings, how slow the taxis taking you toward love, how cold the cold of a running stream, and, in spite of

117

Stevie Crane, how well you will know the color of the sky!

What, though, if the character is Ernest all the time? What if you are not Brett or any of the chaps, what if it is always Ernest talking, Ernest using another mouth to hate Robert Cohn for him, to call him Jew in that mean-mouth tone? Because that is what it was like there in Paris and Pamplona—it was Ernest with something that had been going bad in him for a long time, and now it was working its way out of his book, like one of those pieces of metal he was hit with at Fossalta. A burst of pus, and there it was, that iron junk, his hatred of the Jews that he tried to put inside of me, Mike, Jake Barnes, Bill.

I hate his suffering, I was made to say of Robert Cohn, but I was ashamed when I said it, and it shames me yet. I would not hate a man that I had gone off with and made love to, even if it was unimportant love, and the man was far from my last. I would have a certain respect for what we had done. I would remember what was good about it, and I would forget what was otherwise. Even if it was of importance to him only, and I knew that I would never be with him again, I would not forget what I had felt once, and for that pleasure, I would not return pain. Pain was Ernest's way; it was not mine.

I was thirty-four when he made me Lady Brett, made me his kind of American, and he at the time was twenty-five, young, you might think, but there was much that he already knew and more that he seemed to understand, but there was also much that he did not know and would never understand, and one such thing was women. In that book of his, in all his books, women are the real *toros*, things for men to show their courage against, to make a pure line with, but in the end they are there only to be killed. He liked to kill, Ernest did, and he killed much. Nothing lived that he did not kill, birds, fish, beasts, all women, and himself, finally, but what I hate him for is that he used me to kill the Jew. *I hate him*, he made me say, *I hate his suffering*, but, before God, it was untrue.

Hadley Richardson Hemingway, 1892–1979

THE MOUNTAINS IN THE DISTANCE

She cried and cried and could not tell me.
—Ernest Hemingway

The crying hadn't started when the train drew out of the Gare de Lyon. She was still staring up at the luggage rack, at suitcases, a knapsack, a strapped roll of gear, staring as if at any moment the missing valise might appear, emerge from behind the duffel, show itself, and speak (please God!), saying it hadn't strayed, hadn't been stolen while her back was turned, saying *Here!* Three years of his life would be safe, she thought, stories, poems, pieces for the *Star*, a book that was nearly done. She hadn't begun to cry at Melun nor yet at Montereau. Hope hadn't quite gone as viaducts were crossed, as streams and vineyards seemed to pass, parades of poplars, slowly rising grades—hope was still there through the tunnels, the forests, the black-currant fields. There were no tears at Dijon, there still were none at Dôle. But now in the east, beyond the Franche-Comté, a wave was about to break, the white water of the Alps, far off as yet and faint, a slight disturbance at the base of the sky, and it was only when she saw it that *espoir* became despair. What would she say when he met her at Lausanne? Would she look away across the tracks, the trees, the lake, watch the high white wave, nearer now and poised before the break? Or would she try to speak, try to explain to him what she didn't know herself, why she'd turned her back on three years of his work, lost three years of him? What would she tell him—or would she merely stand there dumb and dumbly cry?

Auld Acquaintance (O. B.), 1928

A POEM SET TO MUSIC

Wenn ich in dein Augen seh'
—Heinrich Heine

The coffin was open, resting on trestles in the middle of the parlor, and from time to time a woman would rise from a ring of chairs and gaze down at the dead, a girl of twenty-three. From where you sat, outside the ring, all you could see above the rim was a small affray of hair, and you stared at it, the last of her, the last, you thought, that involute of hair. You watched the woman reach out and touch it, redistribute it, thin it here and gather it there, and you wondered, as she drew back to note the effect, whether Azrael was now more pleased.

So schwindet all mein Leid und Weh

In the hallway of the flat, there were muted greetings, and from the chairs came upturned looks and recognitions, but you saw no grief, and save for the encircled coffin, the occasion might've been an *evening:* in a moment, you thought, the girl might enter, quite alive, and begin to sing her songs. They were called *Lieder,* she'd told you once, poems in music, poetry sung, and many, she said, had to do with love, bestowed or longed for. The woman was leaning toward the coffin again, changing her arrangement, adjusting strands of hair, and sitting there and mooning the room away; you remembered when a *Lied* had been sung, and its words were meant for you.

Doch wenn ich kusse deinen Mund

You'd been walking with her one night, drifting about the city, and now you were drifting back. Along the way, there'd been talk and intermissions, tangency and distance, chosen words, there'd been care, reserve, avoidance, even, as though you feared some unsound stair. Toward the end, though, you knew that your wandering, however crooked, however aimless, had led to where you were, there on a chance street at an unappointed hour.

So werd' ich ganz und gar gesund

Before, others had always been present when you heard her sing; this time, under some forgotten arc-lamp, she sang for none but you. Your German was poor, but it could've been poorer, and still you'd've known the meaning of the unfamiliar: she made it plain. Her hope was plain too, that you'd tell her, in any language, what she'd just told you. Instead, feeling as if you'd been misused, ill-used, you said *Songs like that make me uncomfortable*.

So muss ich weinen bitterlich

It was said, not sung, and she was dead in one more year. By then, there'd been interventions, as though you'd been going opposite ways in a crowd: people and places had come between you, innumerable words, faces, thoughts, and on other unselected streets, songs had been sung of looks into other eyes. Your mind seemed to come back to you from somewhere, space, night, nothing, and you saw that the room was crowded now. All the chairs were occupied, and callers stood behind them, ranged along the walls. The woman was hovering about the coffin again, and again she was trifling with that little floss of hair. She moved it with deft touches, hardly more than passes of her hand, and then she pressed it down and out of sight, and at last she seemed to be satisfied. You could see nothing inside the coffin now, nothing, and you could no longer stay in the room.

Bitterly. . . .

[*Dichterliebe* #4, by Robert Schumann.]

Auld Acquaintance (S. L.), 1929

THE PLEASURES OF SIN FOR A SEASON

She was waiting for you at the far end of the portico, near the ballroom door. Between you, along the hotel wall, ran a row of wicker chairs and rockers, and there sat elders gazing at the summer night and through it at a host of ghostly summers of the past. There must've been talk, music, laughter, the resonance of footsteps on the porch, but sight diminished sound (the white dress, the black sash, the red rose), and you went seemingly amidst a silence toward the pleasures of the season. In the autumn of that year, there'd be a silence more profound, and mighty men would drown in their deliquescent chink, sink and scream but make no sound, as in a dream of falling. But that time was still in the making, this was the season of sin, and its pleasures wore crepe de Chine, a velvet sash, and a red red velvet rose.

Marian Forrester, in *A Lost Lady* (1923)

A SENSE OF ELATION

She had always the power of suggesting things much lovelier than herself.
—Willa Cather

She was far from Sweet Water, she was in another country when she said to someone *If you ever meet Niel Herbert, give him my love,* and it was done one day, the love so sent was given, but she was dead by then, and the words when heard seemed to drain the air, to make it rare and hard to live on. *Tell him I often think of him,* she'd said, and he felt himself closing, he felt his heart constringe: there was nothing now ahead but the past, he thought, nothing new in the world or even on the way.

He thought of a day in the Forrester marsh. Twelve, he'd been at the time, and he'd seen Ivy Peters stone a woodpecker down and slit its eyes with a blade, and still it'd flown, he remembered with appall, beaten about in the trees, and when it lit at last, it had shaken its head, shaken its head, and many a night thereafter, red and black had come to him in a dream, the red on the run and dripping. That was the day

122

they'd met. *Give him my love*, she'd said in another country far from the Sweet Water marsh, and he seemed to live a little less than he had before.

And there was a day when she'd come to see the Judge, a cold day, it'd been, and she'd worn sealskin with a crimson scarf and garnet earrings, and, watching her, he'd thought of the woodpecker shaking its head, flirting the blood away, dying, and he'd remembered red and black dreams with the red running. *Tell him I often think of him*, she'd said—in what country?—and he wished there were ways of changing chance, rearranging dates and places, encounters, states of mind. *Give him my love*, she'd said, but both had always known that he'd had it from the start.

She died about three years ago. Ed Elliott was saying; *I know that for certain.* But Niel was far away, in another country of the mind, and among the trees of that dream region, her colors, black and red, seemed to flash, and he knew, though he'd never had more than the word, that he'd surely been given all. *Give him my love*, she'd said, and suddenly, instead of shrinking further, something inside him grew.

Willa Cather, 1873–1947

THE LOST LADY

. . . more lost to me than they who dwell in Egypt's sepulchres. . . .
—Willa Cather

They're gone, those letters written by her amorosa. She burned the evidence of fire, ashes now its ash, and, residue herself, she lies where, if such stuff has eyes, she sees Monadnock near, far from the dear sweet mound she'd known for forty years. How had she lasted beyond her truelove's death, how had she passed the days, beguiled the nights, how had she suffered living—had she borne it by reviving a greater pain, the loss of her lady while her lady was still alive?

123

They'd met when young, hardly more than girls, really, and for one at least all the vaults of the heart were filled, and she had no other desire than desire prolonged. And without abatement, without end, it seemed, she'd loved when the two were together, loved while the two were apart, and she'd written of their love and read of it, and neither place nor fame nor time had interfered, and she was, she truly was, requiting her one desire. Would, she must've wished, would that yesterday's round were tomorrow's too!

It wasn't. It ended when her well-beloved betrothed herself to another—and that other one a man! She couldn't bear it (the houses, the rooms, the beds they'd shared, the camping trips, the two alone, and the two on the beach at Le Lavandou, and the two in that chamber at Ravello, where yellow roses framed the window frame), she couldn't bear it, couldn't live with the thought that where her hands and mouth had been, a man's would be, a man's now were!

She did live, though, lived on for thirty years, but she never forgot their early days, their beginning, the part that had promised all.

> . . . *Ah me! I might as well*
> *Covet the gold of Helen's vanished head,*
> *Or kiss back Cleopatra from the dead. . . .*

Auld Acquaintance (R. P.), 1931

A WOMAN ARRAYED IN PURPLE

Jesus Christ, Julian! Don't you know what she is?
—Nathanael West

In the fall of that year, on the roof of the Hotel Sutton, you wrote the first version of *The Old Man's Place*. From there, a dozen floors up, you could see the tip of Manhattan far to the south, the bow of a ship two miles wide and fourteen long, and you'd let yourself suppose that the island was about to sail, was sailing now, moving down-bay toward the Narrows and the sea outside the Hook, a ship of stone on the way—to where?, you'd wonder, and then you were back on a roof, twelve stories up from the street.

You met the woman because of the sun. It was using you as a burning glass, you fancied, and at the point of convergence you'd find its image, a small sun on the tar beyond you, or on the parapet. You turned, but it wasn't the sun that you found, concentrated on some bright button, some round of glass: it was the woman, and lying at her feet was a sheet of paper, one of your pages blown away. Picking it up, you read what you'd written of Harrington Hill—"It was very hot and still, and there was little wind on the east slope. The trees moved only in great sections, slowly, like animals breathing"— and when you looked up, the woman was watching you.

Jesus Christ! Don't you know what she is?

You sat down next to her, recalling the notion you'd had, of the island under way, the city in motion, and you thought of a voyage on a sea without a shore, an endless crossing of a boundless main. You glanced at the glare of paper you held in your hand, and you were about to read aloud from it—*it was very hot and still,* you thought, *and there was little wind*— but in the end, you said nothing and waited for the voyage to begin.

It never began. In the time that followed, you saw her every day and night. You walked bright and dark streets with her, walked streets and parks in the rain. You spoke of things seen and things remembered, of books read and to be written, of the dead you'd loved and the living, of envies, resentments, desires, of yourself and other heroes, and she suffered your talk and listened, as if all you'd said were new. But she never let you touch her, never, and one day, when you tried to call her room, you learned that she was gone.

Jesus Christ, Julian! Don't you know what she is?

But you hadn't known, not till you were told.

Ruby Lamar, in *Sanctuary* (1931)

WALPURGIS-NACHT

*It's not Lee I'm afraid of. Do you think he plays the dog
after every hot little bitch that comes along? It's you.*
                                        —William Faulkner

She was Lee Goodwin's woman, and hovering about the
stove in the Old Frenchman place, she was like a stirring
witch. The fire halloweened her face, tinged it black and tan-
gerine, and it could've been a cauldron that she stood before
instead of a pan of meat, some stew she'd made of merde,
carrion, smegma, a stew for southron fausts. *It's you*, she said
to Temple, the judge's daughter Temple Drake; *it's you*, she
said to the blonde belle of that particular hell, and if the name
Zelda came to mind (*Zelda?*), at once it went away.

Why should she not have been afraid, Ruby with her
dying child, Ruby in her man's discarded shoes, why should
she not have feared that golden crown, those down-bright
legs, the mound where they met (was it golden too?)—why
should she not have said it wasn't Lee, *it's you?* That kind she
knew, and once more *Zelda* (who was *Zelda?*) may have come
to mind. Lee, she thought, remembering. He'd killed a soldier over a Filipino nigger, and to buy him out of jail—fees,
grease, etc.—she'd flashed her tail and sold it by the piece.
Jesus, she thought, *I had three fur coats once.* When she got
him out, she told him how she'd made the money, and though
he'd whaled the whang out of her, he'd also brought her ice.
What good was a woman too nice for her man?

But this one!, she thought, this pretty strip of ass! *I know
your sort. Running, but not too fast!* She was afraid of
this one.

Auld Acquaintance (L. T.), 1932

LET HER TAKE THEE WITH HER EYELIDS

Why don't you practice on a whore?

Your shame deepened the more she hid, or tried to hide, her rage. For some reason, you saw her as a stream, dark Afton, but so far from being stilled by you, she seemed about to flood, to disturb a Mary's dream. She left the bed and crossed the room, but if she'd done so by design, it left her on the way, and she stopped and gazed around her as though to retrieve it from the air. She found nothing, and you thought again of Afton, of green braes drowned and your shame.

Why don't you practice on a whore? she said. Her nipples were hard, clenched, you thought, and they appeared to be raised in anger—pacifiers once, they soothed no more. And there was anger too in her private hair, a black and almost wreathing smoke, and there was anger as sensible as heat in the stare that flared her eyes, and she shamed you when she said what she'd said before: *Why don't you practice on a whore?*

You knew that if you ever saw her again, the words would still be there: they'd never be unsaid, never be withdrawn, they were as irredeemable as time, they *were* time, and having passed, they were forever in being. In the mail that night, you sent her two one-dollar bills, new ones you'd gotten at a store. You hardly knew what you meant. Surely she wasn't a whore. . . .

Unidentified woman, 1936

OKIE MADONNA

Her gown is made of a pair of sacks, ravelled at the edges now and coming unsewn at the seams, and from a throne of torn ticking, she stares past the camera as if the camera

127

weren't there. Held in her lap, a child sucks at a tit showing through a slit in the burlap, and it too stares, not at nothing far away, but at a hated world that begins with you.

[Photograph by Dorothea Lange.]

Mrs. Thomas Eakins, 1852–1938

PORTRAIT OF A LADY WITH A SETTER DOG

"How beautiful an old woman's skin is—all those wrinkles!"

—Thomas Eakins

From the world of the picture, she gazes at the unpressed pants her husband paints in, at the slippers, the underwear, the gallus slung like a bandolier, and she knows that he sees her as she does him, sees her plain face, her odd gown, her barely ponderable breasts, flat ounces, really, where rounded pounds should be. They *see*, these two, she pale, passive, undeceived, he making her thin arms seem to be the arms of her chair.

Looking out, she knows what he sees looking in, what grows upon his easel. No furred and high-world femmes are there, no butterflies affixed to space, no diaphane concealments of the Thames. *Whistler is a great painter*, he'd said, *but for many of his works I do not care*, wherefore she's aware of the company she's being made to keep: gauche and rapt contraltos, oarsmen and monsignori, pale pugs, drained stiffs, fowlers hunting rail. At her feet the setter Harry, in her lap an opened book, but in her mind her husband's work: children playing on the floor, glowing keyboards, glints on glass, on rook and pawn, on a thorn or two in the Nazarene's hair. She knows what there is to be seen in her, shows it, and in his underwear, in his slippers and suspenders, her husband paints it.

"Mr. Eakins, why do you look at me like that?"
"Because you are so beautiful."

128

Curley's wife, in *Of Mice and Man* (1937)

DO YOU LIKE TO FEEL VELVET?

A girl was standing there looking in.
—John Steinbeck

He'd spoken of her before he ever brought her to the door, put the sun behind the cotton dress she wore, made her stop just there, where the outside glare would suede her skin. He'd told of her coming and even foretold her kind, and it came as no surprise that her lips were full and rouged to set off her shadowed eyes, that there was ostrich plume on her mules, that her thin clothes hinted at a spume of secret hair.

And from the very first, he'd been at pains to show the way she'd die: Lennie would merely pinch her head, just as he'd pinched the mouse, and she'd be just as dead. And then, since George would have to dispose of him, the gun had been shown pages back, when used to kill the dog, for which a reason had been found and given: fleas and scratching. It was all there, all planned, and from velvet mouse the trail was blazed to Curley's wife, velvet too.

But why had she been given no name? What was there about the creature (the mouse, the girl) that won her only the right to be thrown away unknown? Why was it *Slim*, why was it *Carlson*, why one-handed *Candy* and the crookback nigger *Crooks*—why those nominations and nothing for Curley's wife? Why was she hated so? What had she done that she deserved to go like that, to lose her life not as *Anna*, *Susan*, *Jane*, but only as Curley's wife?

Elizabeth McCourt (Baby Doe), 1854–1935

THE SEVEN AGES OF BABY DOE
a photographic history

1: Baby Doe as a Young Woman

They were lucky, those who saw her in the round. A downy little creature, she must've been—a peach! a peach!—and she looked, they said, like something painted, but painted from within: they were quite her own, the tone and texture of her skin. It was said too that her hair was in the red range of gold, that it would change light to liquid and purl it among its curls. She was thought to be a flirt.

2: Baby Doe as the Wife of Senator Tabor

When her hair was unpinned, or so her husband claimed, it more than reached the floor: it made a trail for Baby's nightgowns, a tail for Baby bare. The papers called her *plantureuse*, which is to say abundant, and she dressed to show the abundance off. She favored garb that grasped her by the waist, constricted her, served up her breasts, as though for someone's taste.

3: Baby Doe and her Opera Cloak

It was made of ermine, *putorius ermineus*, otherwise known as stoat, and no one remembers how many such died for its shoulder-wide collar, for the dolman folds of its sleeves, the skirts that swept the toes of Baby Doe's shoes. No count was kept of the kills, but against that snow of fur, ninety-seven scuts still show, enough to cry the rank of a dynasty of queens.

4: Baby Doe at the White House

The high world was there to pay its respects to the President's sister, Mary McElroy, but the reports of the day dismissed her as *a small, delicate lady* and gave her space to Baby Doe. She wore for the occasion a gown of black satin with a court train and a corsage cut to flash the gash between her twain of hills. Her Langtry bangs were spoken of, and the ringlets that sprang from her hair, and note was taken of her jet *capote*, her crape veil, and the pansy pigmentation of her eyes. Mention was made of the Senator's millions and of his slapping Chester Arthur on the back.

5: *Baby Doe on a Street in Denver*

At the age of seventy-seven, she was one of several that the camera caught in stride that day on the sunny sidewalk, still for all their show of motion. She was decked in black again, black cotton, though, not satin, and she sported no jet now, nor veil, nor jigging curls below her ear. The silver Tabor millions had gone, and silver Tabor too, and Baby's pansy eyes were a rinsed and wrung-out blue. Her ermine, her golden girdle (a serpent with a ruby tongue), the hundred peacocks that had sprouted from her lawn, all were long years gone. The man ahead of her, the two men behind her, the one in the doorway, none seemed aware of abundance, not there among them on the street.

6: *Baby Doe's Cabin at Leadville (ext.)*

It sat on the slag mounds around the mouth of the Matchless Mine, a one-room shack with a tin roof and windows overlooking ore-car track, tailings, trees in the distance, and distance itself, aglitter as with the fifteen hundred pendants on a Tabor chandelier. There was no paint on the board walls, none on Baby stepping from the door dressed in rags and a crucifix affixed with twine. Seventy-nine, Baby Doe now was, and she had two more years to go.

7: *Baby Doe's Cabin at Leadville (int.)*

They found her frozen to death on the floor. They found her lying among clippings, string, bottles, cans, clothes even older than those she wore. They found her surrounded by pine-bough sprays, a picture of Christ, a wicker chair with bandaged arms, a broken-legged table, a box stamped *Pikes Peak Lard*. They found two dollars.

131

Ellen Lang, 1880 (?)–1935(?)

THE FORM OF A SERVANT

Do all things without murmurings.
—Philippians 2: 14

She came from County Sligo, somewhere on or near the bay, and even now, so late in the day, you can hear her say the name. *Sligo,* she told you, *Sligo,* and the drawn-out word, as ductile as gold, seems air-borne yet. How much you must've heard from her, and how little remains in mind! Just *Sligo* and the cadence of all the rest, a slow glissade of sound.

From the day she landed at the Battery, she worked without murmurings for your Grandma Nevins, never for anyone else, and she held the old one's hand on the day your Grandma died. Between those two days, there were twenty years, and she spent them at the stove and the sink and over cauldrons of clothes, spent them in smoke, grease, steam, suds, and when she chased dust, she was Death so wroth that it fled before her, appeared to disappear. She came from Sligo—*Sligo,* she said—to serve the Jews for twenty years.

One Jew, though, she served all her life—Him who bled above her bed. You didn't quite know why (was it because He was dead?), but the little pink figure frightened you, pink with runs of red, and when you looked at her nailed-up Master nailed up on a wall, you wondered about many dim things, and none became clear. If she'd hated you for the spikes and thorns, you might've seen more than a fearsome figurine.

But she didn't hate. She loved, loved all much and your Grandma most, and you can see them still, bent over tea, intent, thief-thick, the worn old Jew and the round young mick, their voices blurred to surds of sound, a Litvak madonna and a child who'd played by the Moy.

She left after your Grandma died, made her savings do, paid her way in some household—a nephew's, it may have been—and you remembered learning that now she was dying, cancer, her kinsman said, but you were not there, not there holding her hand, not there, and then she was dead.

132

A NINE-PAGE LETTER

I know absolutely what is best for me, and I am completely selfish about it.

Dear Julian, she began, and ink flowed in phalanges, phrase on phrase it strode without a falter across the page. *You can't realize how I feel about the sudden change in our relationship*, she said, and her lines dressed left and dressed right, and in her white and private spacing, words never mingled, letters never met. *Somehow you came to believe in a possibility that does not exist*, she said, and now, like some hostile force, a grammar of cases, genders, tenses, moods seemed to be advancing against you in open order. *Knowledge of myself made me long ago invent a pattern for my life*, she said, and her words were then upon you, trampling, and in their tread was your doom: *Your way of living could bring me only very great misfortune.*

The letter might well have ended there, at the foot of the second page. Whatever it had to tell *Dear Julian* had been told by then, and more would overfill the already full and merely spill away. But more there was for seven pages, and you wondered (you wonder still) what made her waver so, what turned her corps of clauses to a crowd. The writing sagged and climbed now, lagged behind, ran ahead, floundered, fell, and, fallen, died. There were crossed-out dead on every page, corpses hastily buried, as by an army in retreat. There were swarms between the margins, a last stand of words, it seemed to be, a Thermopylae. . . .

You never replied, you never called again—but is that what she wished, is that what the seven pages were meant to do? *I know absolutely what is best for me*, she said, but was she trying to persuade herself in the pages sent to you?

Louise Bryant, 1890(?)–1936

THE WIFE OF JOHN REED

The water he drank was full of little songs.
—Louise Bryant

In the varying stories she told, she was always vague about her time and place of birth, and no one was ever certain of her origin and age. When the facts went up in Frisco smoke, she was free to find new fancies in the ash, and in time she herself may not have known how old she was or even whence she came. There was vagueness too about the way she ended, as though she alone knew the truth and lied. Some say she died climbing a flight of stairs to her flat in Paris, and some say she was coming down, drunk and naked (*prostituée!*) and offering herself on every floor. In between those obscurities, there were five clear years, the ones she spent with Reed; for the rest, she was never quite alive.

It might've been better if she hadn't met him, hadn't been drawn by the light he brought: she had a glow of her own, she thought, and she didn't know that he was the lantern and she what the lantern lit. They were luminaries both, she supposed, wherefore when she ran off with him, she too began to write. It came, alas, to little, to nothing, really: like a candle in a mirror, her candle power was nil. *The water he drank was full of little songs*, she said to someone, but the words were his, and by then he was dead.

In a Moscow hospital, it took typhus two weeks to kill him. A chill at the beginning, and with it rigor and prostration, and then the fever came, seven degrees too high, and the quickened pulse of a failing heart, and the orange-yellow urine, and now the dark red rash appeared, and the blisters of blood, and lastly the open-eyed coma, during which he died. *The water he drank*, she said.

In snow and rain, she followed his coffin to the Kremlin wall, and there it was put into a grave, spoken over, strewn with flowers, covered with earth, and little by little its light grew fainter, and when it failed at last, she glowed no more, ended as he did, in the cobbled square. They were a waste, the sixteen years she wandered toward that flight of stairs, where some say she was going up and others coming down. . . .

Bessie Smith, 1896(?)–1937

DREAMS OF FLIGHT

Oh me, oh my, wonder what will my end be?
        —Bessie Smith, in *Wasted Life Blues*

She really didn't have to sing a song of wonder: her end was in her beginning, and she knew it all along. Born in the barracoons of Chattanooga, she never doubted that though she fled them early, they'd dog her late, and she'd die where she'd lived, in the same or a similar ghetto; it'd be as if she'd been on the run only to stay in one place. And she was right, the worn-out skinful of gin: torn to pieces in a Mississip car crash, she bled, it's said, all over the black ward of a white hospital before they tried to sew her arm back on. She died, of course, and she dwells now in some condemned walk-up in a slum of Heaven. *Oh me, oh my, wonder what will my end be?*

From there, she mourns that wasted life. In a hundred and sixty blues, black and bottomless sloughs of grief, her slurred elegies quaver, her lament for strayed lover and love betrayed, for hard times and harder coming—struck copper, that voice of hers, and listening, you forget to swallow, and for a little while, you think you feel what she does; for the length of her dirge, you're black.

They were driving very fast out of Coahoma that night. She may have been ginned, and she may have been singing something lordy-lord, maybe just coming to that line, *Oh me, oh my*—and there was that truck parked in the road. *Oh me, oh my.*

135

Harriet Monroe, 1860–1936

ON A VISIT TO AREQUIPA

High in the azure steeps. . . .
            —Hart Crane, in *"At Melville's Tomb"*

What an odd place for her to be—Peru—how far from
her Chicago! Seven thousand feet up from the sea, she lies at
the foot of greater heights: Chachani, Ampato, El Misti, three
miles more these Andes rise above the stone above her grave.
Did she regard them before she closed her eyes, those snowy
cerros against the skies? Were they there outside her window,
a poster in its frame? Did she think she might've touched
them, given the power to lift a hand? How strange that she
died where she did, *high in the azure steeps* of Peru, how
strange that she sleeps in Peru!

He'd sent her the poem for her magazine, and on reading
its sixteen lines, she'd found none that she understood. Un-
poetic, she called herself when she wrote to him wondering
how the dice of drowned men's bones could *bequeath an em-
bassy,* how a portent could be *wound in corridors of shells.*
To her, such figures of speech were as frosted glass: shapes
and colors could be seen to pass, but, beyond what light and
motion meant, no meaning could reach her through the
screen. And he replied, trying to gloss what to him was clear,
to dissect emotion, calibrate metaphor, to say in prose the
things he'd sung. He failed, she said: the poem was stiff with
thought, its phrases were tortured, its beauty lost. . . . And
yet, she printed the poem!

And that is why it doesn't matter, the place she chose to
lie. Among the orange trees and the granadillas, she sleeps
against the azure steeps of Peru, a long way from her Chicago
and his drowned bones in the Florida Current, but it doesn't
matter: where they are, the far apart are near.

Edith Wharton, 1862–1937

NARRATIVE IN THREE PHOTOGRAPHS

There was a Wolf under my bed.
—Edith Wharton

1: at five

She wears a white dress and black shoes, and on the black and white squares of some studio floor, she stands like a piece on a chessboard, a little black and white china queen, and straight ahead she stares, all eyes at all that lies before her, a figurine (at five) about to be moved, about to come alive.

2: at seventeen

She's posed against a painted fence in a backdrop drift of snow. She's seventeen now, in black that seems the blacker for the white stuff on her muff and gown, the scrim of flakes in the gallery air. Her gaze is slightly wide of you, a place or two aside from where you stand, and from the expectancy on her face, someone might be coming and not yet be in sight. You wish you were he; you wish she'd turn that look to you.

3: at twenty-seven

The blacks and whites are grays, and no longer is she the little queen made of china, the waiting young lady of the winter-spangled scene. Whatever was coming came (*there was a Wolf under my bed*), and holding two Pomeranians on her lap, she sits there staring, dead.

Unknown girl, Carmel Highlands, 1938

SOMEONE NAMED ANNE OR ANNA

She hailed you along the coast highway near Yankee Point. She was standing in a slough of cones and catkins under a redwood, and when she saw that you were stopping for her, she took up a small valise and came after the car through the henna dust at the roadside. You drove for some way before she mentioned her name, but you heard it inexactly, and you called her Anne at times and at others Anna. Nothing about her actuated interest. Her face was plain and her figure ordinary; her voice, in the head register, wore on the ear; and since she spoke in narrative mainly, her mind seemed matter-of-fact. She was no less indifferent to you, and talk soon became discontinuous, and for miles together there was none at all. To you, she was merely a passenger, someone (Anne or Anna) on the seat beside you, and you'd ride with her for a certain number of hours and forget her when they ended. What you didn't know, when you stopped for her at the Malpaso bridge, was that you were making her part of your life.

You had three hundred miles to go, and if she stayed the distance, you'd say goodbye at your door, but you didn't know the future, not at Peak Immanuel, not at Yellow Hill. You'd've said, if you'd thought, that you'd wave your hand, as she'd done to you, that a meeting on the road would be over with a so-long on the street, but you didn't know then, at Piedras Blancas, that you'd see her again in the coming year. She'd be waiting on your steps one night—Anna, was it, or Anne?—and she'd look like something left there deliberately, gotten rid of, and she'd seem even plainer than before, drearier, a more shopworn Anne or Anna, and without knowing why, you'd ask her in.

You didn't know you'd do that at Salmon Creek, didn't know so far away that she'd have a new story to tell in that head voice of hers, a story of another ride on another road—and love. And you didn't know, at Constantine Rock, that her story would end, all love would end, with a lesion on her lip.

You didn't know that for some reason (what reason?), she'd have to speak to *you* of her sweetheart's spirochete. You didn't know, so far back, that you'd fail her, but you know now that you did.

Oh, *it's gone*, she said, *I'm cured*, but you'd stopped being receptive even to her words, you'd become encapsulated in a membrane of fear, and through it you could hardly see her, hardly hear, and she must've wondered as she went away why she'd sought *you* out, why she'd thought you'd do. You never saw her again, and you've always wondered too.

Elizabeth Drexel Lehr, c. 1875–1940

HARRY DIED IN BALTIMORE IN 1929

I was in Paris.
—Elizabeth Drexel Lehr,
"King Lehr" and the Gilded Age

His dying didn't end their marriage: the marriage had never begun. *You are repulsive to me*, he told her on the wedding night, and so she remained for twenty-eight years, till locomotor ataxia? paresis? put him in his grave. By then, whenever compelled to look at her Boldini oil or the drypoint made by Helleu, she felt that the image was viewing the sitter, that it was seeing what Harry had seen her become with time, an eyesore, a slum. On such occasions, she may have remembered their first supper, when she'd worn for him her rose brocade, made a single bloom among the sheaves of those that were laid about the room. She may have seen one more time the silver, heard crystal and china chime. She may have fancied what she'd fancied before—themselves, the two, the twain entwined. . . . And then he'd said *You are repulsive to me. Women are repulsive to me.* She'd wondered till she died why she'd borne so long the death of pride.

139

Nancy Astor, 1879–1964

MISTRESS OF CLIVEDEN

Oh, Miss Nancy! You'se sho' outmarried yo'self!
> —Liza Piatt (Aunt Liza)

Liza's Miss Nancy was born a Langhorne, but the name, even in the Old Dominion, invoked no magic nor drove it away. Up and down the River Dan, it was mentioned now and then, but nothing signal ensued from the utterance: no thunder was heard in the field, no wonder wrought in the town. It was equally without witchery in Boston, where Miss Nancy's first husband hailed from. A Beacon Street Shaw, the fellow was, scion of the white colonel (fie and faugh!) who'd led the black 54th Massachusetts against Fort Wagner and fallen within sight of Sumter. On her wedding night, Miss Nancy may have thought of that, and thought of it again on the next, when she fled the bloody bed of Bobbie Shaw. The drunkard! the beast!—she may have wished him as dead as the colonel, buried with his niggers on a Carolina beach.

She made a second try with Waldorf Astor, Viscount-to-be and coming master of Cliveden, and, pictures being shown her, Aunt Liza cried *Oh, Miss Nancy! You'se sho' outmarried yo'self!* The lawns and terraces, the pilastered walls! the Louis Quinze ceiling, the tapestries, the inlaid halls! the marble floor and balustrade, the furniture made for de Pompadour! *Oh, Miss Nancy!* said Aunt Liza, but what if she'd read the book of Guests, known the titles that went with the names, heard the badinage at table and the treason under the trees? What would she have thought of the going creed—one Mind, one God, one Christ, and nothing real but Mind—the blind belief of the rich? What would she have felt about such philes of themselves and phobes of the rest, all those lovers of Jesus and haters of the Jews? Would she still have exclaimed *Oh, Miss Nancy!*, or would she have wondered why something seemed to remind her of the colonel, buried with his niggers in a ditch?

Aimee Semple McPherson, 1890–1944

SISTER

I wonder, when we die, if we will be riding around in airplanes.

—last words

She died on her fifty-fourth birthday. The night before, she'd taken pills to bring on repose, and taken more when she was nodding, and in the end she was asleep in bed and awake in Heaven, smiling down on those who'd found her, breathing still but as good as dead. She was no longer wondering about those airplanes—she knew. And maybe she'd always known.

She'd never studied God at school, hardly gone to school at all, knew little of the Lord, less of course than her betters, who'd crammed for the ambo and were destined for the Cross. At ten, she was a rather dear little girl, dressed in velvet and holding a tambourine; at sixteen, the Spirit having given her utterance, she spoke in tongues. Glossolalia ceased only with the pills. Husbands, lovers, children, illness, none of these stilled her, nor spite, nor ridicule, nor even the puissance of the law, nay, not her million miles of going in the world and the million coming back: her mouth was yet in motion when death took her breath away, killed her.

Maybe she's riding around now in some celestial machine, and maybe from up there, dressed as an admiral, a fire chief, Priscilla Alden, she's ringing the jingles of an astral tambourine. Who can say? And maybe she's heard down here by her turkey-necked congregation, her old fools, her old dupes, who'd given her their gold teeth, their wedding rings, their silverware and cash because she'd given them gold and silver once and never sounding brass. Who can say?

She can say. Wherever she is, she wonders no more about those airplanes—she knows!

Zelda Fitzgerald, 1900–1948

THE FICTION OF F. S. FITZGERALD

I recognize a portion of an old diary of mine, and scraps of letters which sound vaguely familiar.
    —Zelda, reviewing *The Beautiful and Damned*

She was wrong, though. He hadn't pilfered her from life and put her into books; much more nearly, it'd been the other way around. Long before he met her, he'd known her in romance, made her to his own imagined measure, designed her looks and manner, her tone of voice and walk, even, one might suppose, her wayward ways, her craze. Thus, when he saw her first—on a dance floor, it was—she seemed to have *become*, to have exuded from his head, an ideal realized; she was the word made flesh, full of grace and truth, and he beheld her glory. A marvel, it must've been to him, another parthenic birth, that there before his eyes was what he'd conceived behind them. Forthwith he crossed the room to his creation, spoke to her and heard her speak to him—and the two were off, a twain on the way to where the way narrowed to nothing, ended for him in squander, for her in fire.

Like her, it sometimes seemed, he too had effused from his fancy, and while they lived, the dreamer and the dreamed, they lived where they belonged, on the page: they always rode the roofs of taxis of the mind. It might've been some feigned operetta they were playing—he champagned from slippers what time she shimmied shoeless, shook her tits on tables at the Ritz. They swam in fountains, shucked in public places, sprouted green and yellow money from their clothes, they were blatant, late, and drunk at shows, wrongheaded in lobbies, bars, cars, and homes, they burned curtains, beds, furniture, turned on taps and forgot to turn them off, they broke lamps, glass, plaster, brought down chandeliers, they drank, drank, laughed and drank some more. They were personae, those two, and their habitat was print.

He managed, through a twenty-year haze, to set that

world down, and when the paper place was made, they went there, he from where he lay on a floor, she from a sanatorium blaze.

Wallis Warfield Simpson, 1896–

THE SHOPPER

My father's health was delicate. He died five months after I was born.

—Memoirs

Some say he was gone when she came, and she knew no more of him than his name on a grave; they claim too that she first saw light from a four-story house in a Baltimore row and not from a cottage at Blue Ridge Summit; and no few fix on '90 as her year of birth instead of '96. Disjoined now the wheres and whens of her earlier days: dates seem to drift among shifting places, and her beginnings are dim, like a dream in the making. In pictures, the cottage and the row-house still exist. One is frame, a gaunt and indrawn figure that trees trick out in prints of leaves; the other is stone, with square windows, one-way eyes that stare outward, as if at passing merchandise. In her childhood photos, she resembles those tenements—spare, constrained, quadrilateral—and, growing, she never outgrew the likeness. She was always a closed anatomy, with the same unnavigable mind. A queer thing, that gaze of hers, lidless and persistent but void of hunger, chill, reptilian, almost, a look bespeaking the will to acquire, to take in whole (a toad, a rodent, another snake), but without the joy, the juice of desire. A shopper, she is, and from a row-house street in Baltimore, from a Blue Ridge cottage, from beds in Pensacola and flats in Coronado, she scrutinizes merchandise.

Emma Goldman, 1869–1940

CASTLE-BUILDER IN UNION SQUARE

The waving of their oustretched hands was like the wings
of white birds fluttering.

—Emma Goldman

At the end, the crowds were only apparitions, the smoke
remainder of a stroke at seventy, shades of the furniture in a
burned-out brain. And yet, how like they were to the crowds
at the start, waiting for her in the Kovno air, there at partu-
rition—the reaching hands, the beating wings! They must've
governed her, those auguries, drawn her toward the Square.
Mystery codes her: there's no way to construe her choice of
roads.

Can we say it was due to her being plain, a five-foot Jew
with light brown hair and *pince-nez* worn on a chain? Or that
it was because she had TB at times, sugar in her urine, an
inverted womb, and a tendency to fall? Would such things
ravel out a taste for pain, would they gloss her lifelong suicide? Would we know her if we knew of the varicose veins,
the broken arches, the throe she had every twenty-eight
days? Would it sink in then why nothing swayed her, nothing
changed her mind or ways, neither the fines she paid nor her
days in jail, not spite and exile, not the poison penned her,
the spew from the pulpit, the dead cats we threw—would
light be shed and she become clear? Or would she stay a
cipher, a disarray of symbols, a lock that lacks a key?

When no one would rent her a room (free lover! anar-
chist! antichrist! suffragette!), she slept in whorehouses and
other public places—streetcars, doorways, toilets in the
park—and when horseshit hit her soapbox, she kept on talking and spoke it away. For those she prized—the poor, the
put-upon, the ill-used—she went to the stake and lit her own
fire. She gave up family, easy money, and the right to come
and go, she gave up fashion, honors, nationality, even, and
finally the quiet and crayon hours of old age. There's no un-

riddling that, there's no seeing around the corners of such a heart.

A fat little woman, she grew to be. Her glasses were thicker than before, and she wore them with temples instead of a chain, and she was shorter by an inch or more, and her lungs were scarred, and there was still a trace of sugar in her water, and her legs seemed stuffed with worms. A big-tittied little dame in a dime bandana and a hand-me-down, a sick old soul, and, damn us all, only yesterday she was stumping for Man out there in the cold! We'll not know why. We'll not know why.

We let her come back to God's country when she died of that punctured artery. We opened the door a crack, about wide enough for a fat little coffin, and she came from the outside world to lie at Waldheim, near those Hunkies we hanged for the Haymarket. We'd rented her a room at last.

Florence Kahn Beerbohm, 1876–1951

THE FIRST LADY MAX

Tell me, when you are alone with Max, does he take off his face and reveal his mask?
                                                            —Oscar Wilde

He didn't put the question to her, of course—she had yet to arrive from (where was it?) Tennessee. Nay, the query was made of someone else, and he was years dead by the time she came—still, why might he not have spoken from the grave, said quite the same from Père Lachaise (*Tell me, when you are alone with Max. . . .*)? And if he had, and if she'd heard, she'd've answered how, how would she have told of a life spent in the shade, a lifelong sense of cold?

Alone with Max: she must always have been alone with Max. He was bright, brilliant, even, and she dim, withheld, seen but rarely and then in black. He laughed much, often at nothing known and sometimes to himself; she was staid, fretful, imposed on, but ever the imposure seemed to be her own. An actress (Mrs. Elvsted, Ase, Rebecca Gamvik), still she was a shy little thing, ready to flee at a sound, indeed, flying, for in Max's pen-and-inks, she was free of the ground, borne by the wind. *Very dear little friend*, his letters began, and she kept them through a courtship that lasted seven years, but who can say what she called him?: he threw her screeds away.

And yet it was past all doubt that he loved her, not with heat but gently, as became a gent, without a bead of sweat, and if she cared more intensely, she hid her fire from his lack of it, burned behind his back. She disliked his friends, was ill at ease with wit and teasing, let him go his way—and how often, it seemed, he went. What she did while he was gone, how she spent the day, to whom she spoke in Rapallo, or even in the Cotswolds, who now can say?

Dearest little friend, he'd write, and *Darling little friend*, yet what did it come to in the end but her cry out across the Genoa road and down to the midland sea: *I am a most unhappy woman!* she said, and why did no one ask her why? The sun shone on the little villa, but there was a chill upon the air, and one day she died up there among the fruit trees, the *sweet darling love*, and cremation having warmed her, she was rowed out across the bay of Tigullio, the little Jew lady, and dropped into the blue gulf, star-of-David blue.

Edna St. Vincent Millay, 1892–1950

DEAD LETTER FROM A DEAD LOVER

Life is . . . a flight of uncarpeted stairs.
                    —Edna St. Vincent Millay

I wish I could keep you from climbing those stairs. I wish I could make you stand where you are, holding that glass and watching day break through the wine, your mind still filled with the night's reading, still given over to defeat in war, to wandering men, love's despair, and the birth of Rome—vergilian. I'd stop the sun, hold it not quite risen, so that morning, ever coming, never came. I wanted much the same once before—in another war, it was.

We remember, you and I, but you with such particularity that it goes beyond recall. That one day (and one was all)—it seems to replay itself for you, or, better, to run like time unused, and yet you've used it in a new way every day of your life. How many words you've spent on those few hours! how many lines to a passion unpent only once! One conjunction, we had, and you've been fertile ever since, an ovipositing bee.

I felt a less incessant itch. A soldier bearing dispatches, I dealt with martial secrets, the fates of other Troys, wherefore if you thought me hardly aware of your hands (too small for an octave!), of you yourself as small (five feet only!), of the red in your hair when lights across the street lit the room—if I struck you as half-alive while you were half-dead, dwell on the phrases you last night read, on arms and Helen and topless towers, and forgive. I did hear the *sunt lacrimae rerum* you expired at the crux, but my mind was on a later war.

It was years before we met again, and though I was still your lover, you by then were my friend. To cover the years, we'd written to each other in print, told all there was to tell of our one and only day, I in my measured way, and you in yours, proclaiming. (In passing, may I say you said *I* too often, personified too much, let the outside world go too far in, rhymed where you might've shaken free of it, might've taken the pins from your hair, and would you not have been well with fewer *ah*s, my dear, and not so many *ohs*?)

But those are things of long ago and gone. What matters now is now, and I want to keep you where you are, holding that wine-glass up forever to a red morning, and never setting foot on the stairs. I wish I could stay you, I wish I knew how to preserve you there—because when you start to climb, you'll die. On the fourth tread, the sixth, the seventh, you'll suffer a throe that'll bar your breath, and you'll set down the

147

glass with care, sit a step below it, and a step below it die. Death, my one-night dear, is also a flight of stairs.

Rosie Ackerman, c. 1885–(?)

FROM THE OLD COUNTRY

Ich arbeit mit das Feuer.
—Rosie

She was a cook in your aunt Sarah's household, and you've never known when you first became aware of her: she seems to have been there before memory, tender of the fire, the fire itself in her savor of smoke. But she was not as graceful as fire, not as spry or variable: she was loose matter, bulk that might've been cast aside at creation as stuff too limp to mold, to hold a cut or camber. On her ramshackle feet, she always wore a man's shoes (whose?), and she rocked as she walked, rather like some jumbo windup toy.

She was a Lithuanian from somewhere along the Niemen, Grodno, it may have been, and unable to read or write in any language, she spoke a broken Yiddish that to you was mainly sound. Your aunt, though, was quite at ease with the greenhorn's locution and shared her stories' blues and highs, wept when weeping was called for, laughed, frowned, expressed surprise. You heard her as through a wall that leached her words of meaning—and you were the wall, you sometimes thought, yours was the mind that couldn't be reached, *you* were the greenhorn.

You can't recall her as a constant, always there and visible: she comes back in discrete appearances, and you think of her life as having been spent only in your presence. And yet in one of its intermissions lay all she ever lived of it: there a son, sole memento of a husband on the run, there her one-year history. And so she looms and sinks away, and time goes in smoke and stories, in broken Yiddish and the pain of broken feet, and one day, at the end of some old-world Megillah, she told your aunt that she wanted her wages, accruing then for thirty years. Asked why she suddenly required all those thousands, which, let her be reminded, were being hoarded against the infirmities of age, she made it known that they were for her son, a baker's apprentice, and that he, such was the loving nature of his heart, would provide the wants of her latter days.

Her bankbook was put before her, its pages dark with deposits (there were no withdrawals), and the sum at the foot of the final column was translated into Yiddish—there lay her earnings in the basement's gloom, standing before the flame, invested with fumes and steam. They were safe where they were, she was told, yet they were hers to do with in such ways as she willed.

But this baker's apprentice of hers, her little Joseph, or Yossele, as she called him, was he wise, she was asked, would prudence guide his use of her thousands? She was shown the sayings of Solomon, and one of these was read to her—*A foolish son is the heaviness of his mother*—and she was besought to consider that Joseph was young and she aging, that her days above the brazen pot were numbered now, that soon, soon, the time of need would come. . . . But if she heard, she gave no heed: despite the Word, she desired her money. May God bless each loaf of Joseph's bread!, your aunt said—and the money was surrendered.

It was a black day. In Joseph's hands, all was lost. The bakery he bought, the stocks of flour, raisins, sugar, the trays and scales and ovens, the sweated thousands, all was quickly lost—a black day! But blacker still the Joseph heart. It lacked, alas, the loving nature that Rosie's loving nature had made her suppose, and when in time her feet played out, she rocked the world away in a home for the aged poor. Truly, even as in Proverbs 10:1, *a foolish son*. . . .

Ella Reeve Bloor, 1862–1951

A SCHOOL FOR YOUNG LADIES
OF GOOD FAMILY

I hated Ivy Hall.

—Ella Reeve Bloor,
We Are Many: An Autobiography

She was a friend of Whitman's in his Camden days, and a queer pair they must've seemed, she barely ten and he five times her age. She'd call when brought to town, and they'd sit on the steps of his house speaking quite as equals spoke, and if the air grew cool, he'd make a cloak of his shawl and share it with the maid. On occasion, they'd walk to the Philadelphia ferry (which one, the Vine Street? the Kaighn Point? the Shackamaxon?), and they'd ride roundtrips all afternoon, holding forth on seminaries, lilacs blooming in a dooryard, brotherly love in the city they were just approaching or about to leave behind. She remembered him all her life, the great gray hat he wore, the gray plaid shawl, the way he'd bare his mind on their crossings of the Delaware. *I see the hurt*, he'd say, *the opprest of the whole earth*, and she'd nod, as though made to see the same, and he'd say *I feel the measureless shame and humiliation of my race*, and she'd be warmed by the words, as by another kind of shawl.

The young lady of good family did not stay long at Ivy Hall, and thus she cost herself the graces of her station, ease of manner, flow of motion, lost the swing and sway that betokened bearing. Never properly now would she descend a stair, sail a room, sit a chair, never learn the pose for pity, horror, pride, aversion, never know the wrong of knowing that the world was full of wrong. She was artless, raw, when she saw the last of Ivy Hall.

Her refinement, when acquired, was the doing of the streets: there, turned, tumbled, collided with, a stone ground by other stones, she was rounded off, she shone. To her, in the war between the states, the states were two, the poor and

150

rich, and as "Mother Bloor" or "that red and renegade bitch," she fought in that war for fifty years. She fought whenever men ate bread in the sweat of other men's faces—she was there, in all those places. She carried signs—*Free Gene!* they said, and *A Living Wage!*—and she walked on lines in the sun, the snow, and rain, and it was she spieling spells from a wagon-tail, a runningboard, a stack of ties, her fist overhead like a torch—bringer of light! giver of fire! ah, she could talk the dead alive, make the dying walk!

From Ivy Hall to the end at eighty-nine, there was nothing for her but *the hurt, the opprest of the whole earth*, wherefore at the last, all might've seemed newly spoken, as if she were still sitting next to an old man in a broad gray hat, still hearing his voice on the deck of a ferry, still being warmed by his words, his mothering shawl.

Grace Hemingway, 1872–1951

MOTHER OF SIX

Some women cling to their husbands . . . some need solitude.

—Grace Hemingway

On the day he shot himself, the doctor had been her husband for thirty-two years. In that space of time, the seven ages of man had passed through the office in his home, and he'd seen the same stages on his horse-drawn rounds. He knew, therefore, the wave of life, the swell, the surge, and he knew too that the wave would break. He'd wrought no miracles in his practice: the hands he'd laid on mortals were merely mortal hands. If it weighed on him that he couldn't cure, could only temporize, he failed to show it, and for thirty-two years, the sick came to his door or called him to their side.

Some need solitude, his wife said, and he may have remembered the comings and goings of thirty-two years, the procession through his office, the children on the stairs, the meals and musicales, he may have dwelt on city and suburban outings, on voices in the hallways, excitement, grief, jeers, prayer, and if the Walloon woods came to mind, he may have thought of crowded tables, rowboats, rooms, limits of pike, grouse, people, of the marraige of his elder son, and he may have wondered whether Grace had been there for those teeming years or always somewhere else.

Some women cling, she said, and toward the end, he may have known that she wasn't one of them, that she was no vine or, worse, that he was no wall, and now with angina, with sugar in his blood and urine, he did rue it that there was no perpetuant power in his hands. Thirty-two years, he may have said to himself in that office off the landing, and taking some papers from his files (which and why?), he burned them in the furnace and climbed to his second-floor room. There he put a Smith and Wesson against his right mastoid bone and put a stop to his years of Grace.

Her elder son asked for the weapon, and she sent it to him, along with a cake and some of her paintings. *Some need solitude*, she'd said, and now at last she had it.

Mrs. Ada Russell, 1863–1952(?)

ADA LIVED TILL ABOUT 1952*

*. . . my love will go on speaking to you
Through the chairs, and the tables . . .*
                                        —Amy Lowell

They'd been lovers for a dozen years when Amy had her stroke and died, and then, though she went on speaking through the relics she left behind—the books and pictures, the paneling, the crystal chandeliers—her wife, her widow, may not have known or heard the dead language of things, and for her life's last third, *till about 1952*, she may have thought herself alone.

None of the Back Bay blues seems to have noted down her day of dying—they let her drift away—but they were quite aware of all the rest, alive to her prior thirds. They knew her naughts and picayunes, and if imprecise on when she went, they could tell you when she came, and they knew as well her father's trade (he sold books, but he did *sell*), nor were they dense about her stage career and blind to her divorce. They were there, of course, there in the very room, when she and Amy met and all but merged, and you'd swear they trailed the pair, lost to Boston, through the Boston streets—they knew it all, they as much as saw it, the coupling of fat Amy and her crimson-buttoned bride. They were there, or thereabouts, for a dozen loving years.

At best, it was only semi-private, that affinity, and there were no doubts among the ladies on the Charles. They'd seen it come into being and watched it on its way, and if they'd wondered how grace coped with mass, they may have remembered cathedrals. Yes, they'd been in on twelve years of Amy ardent, *You spread a brightness where you walk*, she'd said, and *I see your lifting skirts*, and now she was dead, and her heavy ghost rode the air at Sevenels, bestrode the Orientals below the chandeliers.

But it was a pedigreed ghost, *une âme de race*, whereas the body it sought and spoke to belonged to an actress, and a sapphic one at that. It lived, the ladies thought, *till about 1952*.

*Jean Gould, in *Amy* (Dodd, Mead & Co., 1973), p. 355.

Ethel Rosenberg, 1916–53

A LETTER TO JULIUS

An apple seed which I planted, and have watered
patiently, is sprouting bravely.
　　　　　　—Ethel Rosenberg, Sing Sing, 1951

From her cell in the Death House, she was writing a
letter to his, a hundred feet away. A fine rain was falling, she
told him, as if describing another world's weather, and she
spoke of a scent of flowers that came, she almost thought,
from a world that neither knew. She reported damp sparrows
picking at damp bread, dough again, and then she sought a
sight of color, she said, and she gazed at the heart-like leaves
of a wild violet, at a sprig of parsley between a wall and a walk
outside, and at something green that seemed to grow from
the concrete, a verdant inch or two nourished by sand,
gravel, lime, a new and minute tree headed for the sky.

What variety would the pome turn out to be, a rome
beauty, was it, or was it baldwin, pippin, winesap, was it grav-
enstein or oldenburg, and what hue would she see from that
cell, russet red or yellow golden? Would the shoot survive
fungi and viruses, the climate, the soil, would the plant louse
infest it, the woolly aphid, would the codlin moth crack the
rinds, attack the cores, would blight cause the fruit to fall, or
would she never know, having fallen herself before her time
to fall?

Mabel Dodge Luhan, 1879–1962

HOW THINGS DIE ON ONE!

Flowers quickly disintegrate with me when I wear them.
— Mabel Dodge Luhan

She was born in Buffalo in one of those foursquare brick houses on upper Delaware, and a box of marital hatred, it must've been, with her glass-cool mother reading while her father shouted *Whore!* So rank the air with parent poison that light scarcely lit the rooms, but for a score of years, she breathed the fumes of their cold smolder, nor was it pure next door or across the way: immured aversion there as well, and all along that gilt-edge street. Small wonder that she wore out flowers, cost them their color, withered them, and even smaller that she wore out people too, faded them, cankered them, made them dry away. At fifty, she wrote *How things die on one!*, and she looked back through herself to find out why they'd died on her.

She looked back through a *Gran' Salone* ninety feet long, with doors, sage green and gold, from a church in Pisa, finely carved, she said they were, a maze of moldings, she looked back between damasked walls, past tapestries from Flanders, pilasters, brocades, girandoles, down consoled halls she gazed, and saw, beyond Firenze and the Settignano hills, beyond a haze of men consumed and burning women, beyond *the bland and insincere blue sea*, saw Buffalo and the hate-shot houses on Delaware.

She looked back through days of buying, fitting, trying on, through clouds and clouds of clothes, she peered through causes bedded but never espoused, through spates of letters and sprawls of talk, all so ill-lit, so unilluminable, really, and there were vague vogues, *peyote*, Macedonian cigarettes, a turbaned swami in an apricot robe, and a doctor, quite the rage, who stood on his head—literally, my dear—and peddled glass dilators for the rectum, singly or by the set.

She was, as she said of someone else, *so at home in her-*

self, that when she looked back on lack of love, she did not see her own. There were her beginnings, bricked in along Delaware, street of blinds drawn on frenzies and spite, on chattels and expectancies, on food, fashion, repetition, plans for travel (with pony, cart, and maid) to nowhere and return. Small wonder that the people she picked went dry on her, like the flowers she wore, lost their color, blew away.

How things die on one!

Agnes Smedley, 1894(?)–1950

BY THE TIME THIS REACHES YOU

I will be with the Eighth Route Army.
—Agnes Smedley

She said she came from northern Missouri, but she didn't quite say she was born there—on occasion, talk was heard of Oklahoma—but one or the other, or even Colorado, where her father left some traces, the place is hardly worth a mention; it doesn't matter. What does is where she ended, where the landless lady lies. Forget the locus of beginning, a rift between two thighs, forget the name of the state and town (Osgood, was it?), the shanty between two creeks, forget the wash her mother took in, the smell of sweat and brown soap boiling, forget the poor fist and the poorling fare, the rare term at some far-off school, forget the hired-girl and hash-house days, the tobacco she stripped by hand (six million miles of strings!), forget the daughter's wanderings, the strange lands, the stranger ways, forget all but the yellow faces and the home she finally found. Though she'd dwelt in many a country, she lived in only one, and, dying outside it, she begged to be buried within, and it was done. She's among those she marched with once, and near Peiping, on marble above her dust, she's called *a friend of the Chinese people*.

How many friends to have made, how many friends . . . !

156

Aline Bernstein, 1882–1955

A LINGERING ILLNESS

How shall the years pass, Jew?
>   —Thomas Wolfe

The books about him end on a hillside in Carolina. They
tell, in their closing pages, of some plague that went to his
brain, tubercles like millet seed, it's said, and they tell of
pressures within his head, of pain that led to trepanation,
coma, pneumonic stertor, and then death that came when no
one, kin or friend, was with him in the room. They speak, all
those books, of his outsize coffin, imported, for there was
none to fit him in Baltimore, and after a train-ride to the
tomb, they end on that hillside, Tom dead and I with seventeen years to kill.

How shall the years pass, Jew? he said, but he knew,
knowing time, that the years don't pass at all. They grow, the
years grow other years, evolve them from themselves, and
you undergo them like a sickness, as he endured his own, you
make and contain your divisions, your neoplasms, and so far
from killing them, you die of them. When we met, he was
twenty-five and I his mother at forty-three—he himself said
it, *grey-haired, wide-hipped, timeless mother*, he said—but
for a while, I was other things too, his *plum-skinned wench*,
his *Jew*. I wasn't his mother in bed: there I was his spell-
struck glass wherein he saw the Tom he wished, I was his field
of valor, and I showed him victory, I was home.

We were lovers for three years, longer than I'd've
thought at the start but at the end too short by far. By then,
I was greyer-haired, wider-hipped, timeless no more, and
though I tried to bring them back, our lover days were gone.
I wept, I clasped him and conjured him, I bought him gifts,
pursued him with screeds, stood before his door and besought him from the street. Greyer by the day, wider, more
and more mother, I threw pride away and proffered money.

His real mother was there for that, and she laughed at the notion: her Tom being paid by a Jew!

How shall the years pass? he said, but they haven't passed yet, they weight me from within, stones grown by other stones. Ah, Tom, so strong, so strong, and gone so fast—and I lasted! If there'd been a way, I'd've given my un-passed years to him, I'd've died for him, his Jew.

Zora Neale Hurston, 1903–60

A PILGRIM TO THE HORIZON

I have been a Negro three times—a Negro baby, a Negro girl, and a Negro woman.
　　　　　　　　　　　—from *Dust Tracks on a Road*

Her papa, John Hurston, was a cotton-chopping nigger from Notasulga, which it is in the state of Alabama between the Tallapoosa River and nowhere in particular. A stud-looking buck, he weighted in at near about two hundred, and being light in color with gray-green eyes, he might've had some dicty blood, Creek, maybe, or maybe even white. Her mama lived higher up the hill, much too high for a landless cropper with fadedy skin: black, thin, and ninety pounds of pretty, Lucy Ann Potts was not for such as he. Still and all, what's too low to love?—and down the hill she ran to lay her hand in John's. Her own mama never forgave her for that: to her, the man was always *that yaller bastard.*

He was off running the roads when Lucy Ann's water broke and flushed out Zora Neale, and all the woman could do was lay there in the wet with the kid betwixt her knees till finally a white neighbor chancied along and cut the cord with his Barlow knife. Next thing she knew, he was sponging the slick off the child and tying on a belly band, after which he mouthed John for not being there, and he stomped out all clouded up and trying to rain. A wrathy old feller, but he didn't fool Lucy Ann—he didn't even fool Zora Neale, and she an hour old. How could he? The first thing she saw in the world was a veal-colored man washing off her feet all gentle and Jesus-like, and her life began free of gall, free of fury.

Her mama taught her to jump at the sun—you mightn't land there, she was told, but you'll get off the ground. And her mama said *Don't squinch your spirit*, which was a good thing too, one of many that the little body knew. And then she died, and for Zora good things ended at the age of nine. At fourteen, she left home, a pilgrim bound for some Palestine, a peregrine for Rome.

Manicurist, waitress, backstage do-all, watcher of sickbeds, she was, and student in between, anthropologist, collector of folkways, and lastly writer of books, always on the wander, never here for long or long where she went—pilgrim to the horizon, and to the one she saw from there. *Ships at a distance*, she wrote, *have every man's wish on board*, and she wrote this, *There is always room in oblivion*, and she wrote this too, *I have been in sorrow's kitchen and licked out all the pots*, but toward the end she wrote no more. She was a lady's maid again, and after a stroke she died broke in a Florida hospital, and they had to pass the hat around to box her and put her in the ground.

From down there, she may have spoken upward once, to say very softly, *I have been a Negro four times: I'm a Negro in the grave.*

Mrs. Woodrow Wilson, 1872–1961

THE WELL-DRESSED DEAD

This pleasant place formed a retreat in which to rest after a sea trip, and afforded an atmosphere of quiet and dignity which I loved.

—Edith Bolling Wilson

When her *Memoirs* came, he was a dozen years on the way to dust under a marble flagstone in the floor of a cathedral, and, strange, how meet for cankered Woodrow her winding sheet of words! They wrap him round against the cold, they help him hold his bones in place, they keep his sunken face from sinking further in. They enclose his rotting clothes, her plies of well-bred language, and most properly dead her Woodrow lies.

How seemly she makes them seem, the twain, how high in mind and handsome! They never fall from grace, the pair, or into graceless ways, and all they say is spoken fair, tendered, really, shy bouquets of thought. How mild they are, how civil, sane, and *comme il faut!* Their griefs are stately and secluded, their pleasures begin and end on the hour, and their passions—but there are no passions here, no people. There are only transparencies, figures moving across a war like double exposures, gauzes as bodiless as those *dear ghosts* he'd mourned, *those dear ghosts that still deploy upon the fields of France.* But there are no people.

Emily Hale, 1891–1969

A THOUSAND LETTERS FROM *OUR FRIEND*

Weave, weave the sunlight in your hair—
—T. S: Eliot

A thousand (some say more), and they're not to be read till she's fifty years dead—by will, she must be dead for fifty years. Only then, if one still cares, may a scholar unlock the vault, unseal the files, the folios, and learn what *our friend*, as she called him, had written for her eye through all those troubled midnights, through the noon's repose. And what will he find, that archivist, what will be there, what more will *our friend* have written of how the sun seemed spun in her hair? What will they tell of *her*, those one-way words he sent—a thousand letters, what will they have meant to her in another country?

Given, her place above him on the garden flight, given too, her armful of blooms (roses, they might've been), but no one knows, not yet, why she flung the flowers down. What had he said from the foot of the stair, what had so surprised her, made her turn, weaving the light in her hair, grieve as he went away? Will the schoolman cull the answer from fifty years of grains, will the answer itself be grained, be dull—will he find that *our friend* had loved, but only in his mind?

Stand on the topmost stair, he said, hold there still, lean just so on the garden urn, weave, weave the sunlight in your hair, grieve as I go, but do not ask that I live in this life . . . is that what all those letters will say?

Dorothy Thompson, 1893–1961

THE LAST TERRIBLE REMEMBERING

Nothing but faint distaste.
—Dorothy Thompson, diary

In the stir and flurry that attended her, in the charged and particular commotion she made, matter itself seemed on the move and she the cause of causes. About her always, a daze of orbits and a monotonic din, like wars of bees, and in their whirl and bourdon, values appeared to change: the mere became the rare and the rare peerless, olympian or very near.

It took time, twenty years, for the sound to die and the stew to still, and only then she knew the mount she hadn't climbed, the divinity she hadn't been. She didn't leave at once. She lived on for *the last terrible remembering*. It came to her in a hotel room in Portugal, it came during the night and through the rain, it came long after the crowds had gone even from her mind, and if she was lucky at the end, she felt nothing at all, or only faint distaste.

Marion Davies, 1897–1961

THE MISTRESS OF CITIZEN HEARST

I loved him for thirty-two years.
—Marion Davies

Thirty-two years, give or take the odd month, and then he was dead, and while she slept, they took his body away— *whoosh*, she said, *and he was gone*. He was ninety or near at the time, and in truth there wasn't much to take, only some shrunken stuff in speckled skin, meat long hung and high. What there was, though, they laid out in a Nob Hill cathedral, where, for two whole days, the great and small came to see what'd made all the fuss and grown so rich on bluster, and when they saw a meager old stiff in dark blue worsted, some of them sighed *Ah, well* and some *The son-of-a-bitch.*

When his heart stopped, she was asleep in an upstairs room. She was dreaming, possibly of him, when his fibrils ended their independent beat, and his blood lay still and lack-luster, like a killed snake. The racket and randan he'd made, the wars he'd caused, the nunneries he'd bought, the tapestries, the Dutch armor, the cannon he'd brought from Morro Castle, all such things no more, no more Steens among the Bouguereaus, no more Delft, Navajoes, Tanagra figurines. While she slept and dreamed, possibly in Richelieu's bed, he died in someone else's, downstairs in another room. The life-long squander was over.

He was dead, and his body was gone, she said. *Whoosh, like that. Old W. R. was gone.* She thought, having loved him for thirty-two years, that he belonged to her, but they taught her otherwise. They bore him away, shrouded him in blue worsted, and showed him off for two days to the small and great, none of whom was she. A fallen woman is all she was, a whore for thirty years and more, well paid for lying down when bidden, the kind to keep hidden when Corinthians was read from and César Franck was played. Her love had been a red-light love, wherefore she was nowhere near when they prayed for his soul as he passed from sight.

I loved him for thirty-two years, she said, but that didn't trouble them. What did, though, was that he'd loved her, and no less long.

Dorothy Comingore, 1913(?)–1965(?)

THE MISTRESS OF *CITIZEN KANE*

You thought, on reading of her death, that little of her had been caught by the words: for all you could tell, they might well have been the vita of an impostor. They gave her

163

descent, her small-town birth (Downieville), and some other-ville where she died, but the names and dates seemed to be those of a stranger, a foreign body that wore her clothes and face. But then, when was she not a strange one? She had no core, no attracting center, and she'd change even as you watched, like a sculpture made of snow: her true being was amorphous.

She made you think of drink, and though you never saw her drunk, there was always something about her that be-trayed the fact of use, something come undone, the loose thread, the stray of hair, the hook that lacked an eye. Some day, you knew, there'd be one too many gaps or junctions one too few, and she'd give way altogether, leaving nothing to show where she'd been but a pool of melted snow.

You stare at her in a pair of photos—in the first, she's the mother, in the other the wife, poses she could hold only for the shutter instant. Apart from such stopped fractions, she was her liquefactive self, dwindling before your eyes. And seeing her that single time on the screen, pretty enough, but green and gaudy, frizzed, bangled, trailing stuff and causing flash, trash, really—seeing her on that one occasion, you be-came aware that she wasn't a player at all. Up there, unreel-ing in black and white, was she. Not some celluloid mistress, off-key singer, futile weeper, wringer of hands, not some flaunted thing of naught, a fiction projected in the dark, but she the real, the unideal she.

You didn't know, watching her filmed disintegration, that she was living her life in advance. There she was, giving you in two hours the twenty-five years to come, showing you her incoherence, her nature's lack of bond, her tendency, her trend toward ending. There, unaware, you saw her long thaw to nothing. The absinthe days were on the way, the street-walked nights, the slubbered rooms with rubber douches on the doors—you could've known of those things if you'd looked with care, and through a barred window somewhere, you could even have watched her die.

Lucy Young, a Wailiki Indian c. 1846–?

LISTEN TO HIM DREAM

My grandpa say White Rabbit—he mean white man—
gonta devour our grass, our seed, our living. We won't
have nothing more, this world.
                        —Lucy Young, remembering at 95*

Her grandpa had never seen a white man, but that was
the dream he had each night, and there were people who
came from far away to hear him dream it, and always in the
morning, some of these would be there to learn what the spir-
its had brought him, and when he told them, they said

Oh, you out your head, grandpa, don't say that way.

But he was very old, with his legs doubled up, so that his
knees nearly touched his chin, and his indigo eyes, deep,
deep, looked not out but in, and therefore he knew well what
things were in the dream, and he said

I not crazy. Young people gonta see this.

And one day he died, and the people tied him in his
deerskin with ropes of grass, and they were about to burn him
when he rolled over and came back, saying he was starved for
water. They gave him the little basket he'd used as a cup, and
he drank till satisfied, and then he died again, and this time
he was placed above the fire, and his basket too, and he went
to where people go when they go at last. But first he said this:

I gonta leave you today. Pretty soon dead. Speak no
more.

She never grew very much—Li'l Shorty, her grandpa
called her—but she knew a great deal for her size and age:

My grandpa put his hand on my head, smoove my hair,
and hold his hand there

*California Historical Society Quarterly, vol. XX, no. 4, Dec. 1941.

and he said,

Long time you gonta live, my child. You live long time in this world.

And she did live long, even as he had said, long enough to see the grass, the seed, the living go, and near the end, blind with cataracts, she still could see back in the black of her mind: she saw the world of her people devoured. And she said,

I hear people tell 'bout what Inyan do to white man. Nobody tell it what white man do to Inyan. I tell it.

And she told it, in nine pages of rude and rending eloquence. She told how the soldiers came to herd her people and how they ran away, told how they slept in the punk hollow of fallen trees, how they ate serviceberries, sunflowers, quamash bulbs when found, pinole from pounded wheat, told how the winds blew and how cold they were in the rain. She told of serpents, bear, danger from the soldiers' dogs, and she told, alas, of being caught, of how they were sold, defiled, beaten for working and beaten for not, and made to watch their men, noosed for hanging, plead to be shot instead, and she saw that done, she said, saw *forty Inyan in a row* shot dead, and she told of the soldier-war wherein her brother was killed, and her father, and her cousin

got shot side of head, crease him, all covered his blood, everything. We helpum wash off. No die

and a young woman

shot through lights and liver. Front skin hang down like apron. She tie up with cotton dress. Never die, neither.

Ah, it was all long, long ago, she said, and all her children were dead but one, dead of the soldiers, of the White Rabbits, of the chest sickness, and now, on the Round Valley Reservation, she lives preacher-married with her husband Sam, a Hayfork Indian:

He's good man. Talk li'l bit different to us people, but can understand it.

And grown old, she knows that her life, like the light her eyes allow her, is dim and ever dimming, and at times she thinks of her grandpa's dream and how it all came true.

That's history. I seen it myself.

Sylvia Beach, 1887–1962

12, RUE DE L'ODÉON

Who is Sylvia? What is she
That all our scribes commend her

—James Joyce, 2 Feb. 1922

Above the windows of the shop, a sign read *Shakespeare and Company*, and she sold books there, books in many sizes, many shapes and colors, many languages, and, bound or *en brochure*, anyone's imprint could be found on her tables and counters and in the stacks that piered the walls, in the tiered racks and rows that started at the floor. Until then, therefore, she was merely a seller of paper, a chapman who'd quit the streets and settled in a store, but on that very day, through the iron frame of her doorway, there came a book in Ionic blue, its title in white letters, *Ulysses*, a writing on the sky, and she, in wandering her aisles, wandered the isles of Greece. How much life there is in books!, she may have thought, and scanning the tapestries they made around her, she knew, she must've known, that there was none like her own publication, the one by the Crooked Jesus, writer on the sky.

It must've been in her mind ever after, behind all she said and did, a presence there in blue, and if she bought and sold as before, if books became cash and cash became books again, if she kept to her usual ways, sat or stood among *all our scribes*, staring at their names, their work, their photographs in frames, if she smoked, spoke to certain patrons and passed some others by, if Adrienne waved from across the street and she at Adrienne, if she continued to walk in her world of print, still she knew, she must've known, that the world was not the same: the Crooked Jesus, his book had changed it.

On an afternoon nine years into that new age, even if she'd glanced at the windows, she'd have made out little through the vapor on the panes and the vaporous rain outside, cars, perhaps, huddled people, stars of light, but she'd not have noted one of the many passersby, seen him stop before the bookshop and look down at a propped-up copy of *Ulysses*, its coloring reversed now, white the cover and blue the title. Her mind was on other things, each more important than a blur on the glass, a shadow, steam, and quite possibly she was unaware when the shape moved and came inside. If it drifted past her, past the crack regiments of the great, if it asked a question and got a reply, if it paused to touch the mantel, dark marble, to gaze at the black stove, the brass urn, the ceramic bust of the Bard, if it slowly flowed back to the door, turned for a last look—*one day*, it may have thought, *one day maybe I* . . . —she hardly knew it was there, never knew it had gone.

Sylvia Plath, 1932–63

TO HER FRIEND, WHO SAID

Then Sylvia was dead. I still don't know the details. They don't matter. . . .

They do matter. If not, she becomes a mere figure of speech, her own, the train that leaves a line of breath: at death, she's no more than that, no mass, she's a blue ghost for the wind to unravel and dwindle away. They do matter. They'll tell, when known, why she could no longer live in the world, given her kind of mind. They'll tell why at thirty-one she found herself done with this place, why the last sound she heard was the sigh of turned-on gas—*alas*, it might've been saying, *alas*, and Sylvia was dead in a little while.

She died in the house where Yeats once lived—see the Wedgwood plaque above the door. Was there something in the air, the walls, the stair that led to her floor? Had something been left behind, his husks and grumes, the chaff of winnowed words, was it the chill that killed her, the coldest London in a century and a half? Or did she bring to those rooms her own killing frost . . . ? They matter, the details. They're Sylvia's chaff.

Flannery O'Connor, 1925–64

THE DEADLY BUTTERFLY

Do not go gentle into that good night
Rage, rage. . . .
—Dylan Thomas

The sickness sets in with a mere heaviness in her arms, as though she were trying to swim in clothes, hardly enough to betoken that she's just begun to die. Nor does the low fever seem to signify, the fatigue, or, more properly, the fatiguability—a malaise is all that all such comes to, an unease of the spirit that soon will pass away. But then they find those broken hairs above her brow, find her toes and fingers cold—Raynaud's phenomenon, they call it—and at last, athwart her cheeks and nose, they perceive the rose-red rash, the butterfly, and, fifteen years before she dies, the cause of death is known.* She knows as well as they, and writing is her rage against the dying of the light.

Her stories are crimes of the blackening heart, murders in words, perpetrations, and they move from start to death without a swerve or stumble, without a moment's doubt. Sitting at a table beside a window, she gazes out over her breviary and missal at a garden where her peacocks preen, parade their iridescence in blue and green and gold, and as if she sees a face in the feathers, a victim, she begins to lay the

169

train for his or her demise. How best, she appears to wonder, how best to do to Mamma and Mrs. May, to Parker and Tanner and Mary Fortune, what life has done to her, and she might merely be choosing a pencil as she compares a stroke with a goring, weighs death by education against a fall down a flight of stairs.

She has been told of spontaneous remissions, of good response to rest, lotions, avoidance of cold, but she believes in no miracle (the missal! the breviary!), no, nor in prodigies from herbs. She believes in accidents, the kind that befell her at twenty-five and that she now has in mind for Tomsee, about to shoot his mother, for Mrs. Turpin and her wart-hog face, for little self-scragged Norton, nearly done with his walk in space.

Rage, rage against the dying of the light.

*Systemic lupus erythematosus.

Elisabeth Morrow, 1903–34

THE FLIGHTLESS ONE

It would be awful if this Elisabeth rumor blew up again.
                    —Anne Morrow Lindbergh, diary, 1928

There was talk about it at the time, and there's talk yet: it was thought once, and some still think it, that he was drawn at first to the older sister, that she was the one who'd caught his eye. If so, nothing came of it, and she was to die in seven years the wife of someone else. Surmise, the notion of a heart forlorn, of secret mourning, of seven years of tears and rue— hearsay all, all of it untrue.

Elisabeth is so wonderful and natural with him.

A suppose, the story was, a bubble that rose through the mind, transparent, rare, lighter than air, but even so it was real enough when it began to be heard, for the source of the word was Anne. *I was sick with envy of Elisabeth*, she wrote, sick of the spell she seemed to cast, her wit and grace, her way of being seen, and it was the last that may have made Anne greenest. *Sick with envy*, she wrote that Christmas Day in Mexico now fifty years past.

Her letters and journals are a partial tour of a private mansion, a roped-off view of Anne. But her older sister has no afternoons when her floors are trod from two to four, and the murmur from within is blood in an unsound heart, a soft wind blowing, the sound seems to be. There's no record, or none yet known, of those seven final years, nothing tells of hopes that went out one by one, of the long extinguishment, the loss of light, nothing tells why the spells failed her, the wit, the grace, her way of being seen. In the end, she was dark, and she simply disappeared.

Dorothy Parker, 1893–1967

THE LONG SUICIDE

Oh, please, please, let her be able to get drunk, please keep her always drunk.
> —Dorothy Parker, in "Big Blonde"

Where she was, there excitement could almost be seen with the eye. Roundabout her presence, a trembling seemed to arise, like an ascension of heated air, and in that fertile element, weeds of wit grew wild. Her sphere fairly shook with *mots* and *jeu d'esprit*, and those who'd rarely shone elsewhere were all but blinding here. They warmed at her appearance, performed for nods, frowns, stares, or nothing, yet they never really knew the five-foot lady Jew: she was public with her person but private with her mind.

Her sun was a burned-out mass of gas, and she dwelt in a blackness so absolute that not even death could've turned it darker, wherefore she tried four times to end her life. But veronal failed to float her off, and the wrists she butchered healed, and four times she awoke in the middle of her livelong night. *Please, please,* she wrote for big Hazel Morse and for a little brunette Jew. *Oh, please, please. . . .*

Ayn Rand, 1905–

SPEAKING AS JOHN GALT:

I will never live for the sake of another.
                              —Ayn Rand, in *Atlas Shrugged*

Forgotten so soon my One begotten that I gave to save the world! So soon lost the sinless Ghost in Mary, the star above the inn, gone the Son, the spangled manger! Null now the Word He brought, the repentance taught at Capernaum, thrown away the Galilean walk and the stilling of the storm! For naught these things, His threefold fall on the road of the Cross, the thorns He wore, the scarlet, the reed He bore in His hand! All for the mockery alone the spittle He endured, the vinegared sponge, the gall! Nothing, nothing, His dying in the ninth hour crying, as David did, *My God, my God, why hast thou forsaken me?*

Not thee, and not David, but this one saying *I will never live for the sake of another,* her I *have* forsaken and forever!

Carson McCullers, 1917–67

THIS SIDE-SHOW

Nature is not abnormal; only lifelessness is abnormal.
                              —Carson McCullers

Somewhere she speaks of those that God never finished, that He'd begun and gotten bored with, freaks He'd thrown away, dumb, deaf, dwarfed, defectives on the way to perfection. The hare-lipped, the club-footed, the strabismic, the zigzaggers of creation, all the askew and bendified, these were the kind that caught her eye. And small wonder why: she was one of them, a freak herself, but a freak inside.

She might've lasted longer if the disfigurement had shown, if she'd lurched, squinted, drooled, worn her tattoos on her face instead of on the lining of her heart. It might've been better if all had seen what she was within, wrung, writhing, dashing at her walls, her own prisoner, like a hunchback. But alas, what rose from that internal churn of hers was a froth of ailments, crushes on womanly men and other women, a love of drink and smoke, falls, fears, blindness, and a stroke at thirty—after which, partly paralyzed, she began to drag a leg. And then at last she was in the open, a freak for this world of freaks to see.

Gertrude Stein, 1874–1946

ALL STIFF AND YET ALL TREMBLING

. . . the suggestive movement underneath the rigidness of forced control, all the queer ways the passions have to show themselves. . . .
—Gertrude Stein

Frying size she never was, not even the day she saw daylight between her mother's thighs. She came out big and biggened by the year, expanded from goodly to gross and kept on thriving, throve until she died. Clothing always seemed in collapse about her, a down and undulant pavilion, and swathed in its folds were the knolls and dales of her rolling hills, the swales where rills ran and mosses grew, but only God and Alice knew those umber places, knew the mauve secrets of the shade. So enwound, she resembled something snared, a gynecomastic male, beamy, ox-hocked to the point of dropsy, with fat little hands like huffed-up rubber gloves: she did not suggest a she.

In the word, though, she's nothing else: she's the good Anna, and she sees the round around her blind with the good-Anna mind and eyes. A surprise, it is, to find her women so nearly real and her men so merely names. You'd've supposed that from such bulk, only the crass and massive would be seen, the occupant things, shadow-makers, shakers of floor and wall, you'd've expected her women to be furs and her men to wear them. Instead, it's a full-breasted world, a world of not-touching men, one where one gender only sways, names the visible, frames the ways—and the other, hardly more than floral, drifts through it like a spore, a lost seed for a lost once-fruitful land. . . . And yet, underneath those clothes, a stir within the stiffness, snows falling in glass balls, swirls alive in amber.

Alice B. Toklas, 1877–1967

PRECIOUS PRECIOUS GERTRUDE

And now she is gone and there can never be any happiness again.
—Alice B. Toklas

There never was a day when she didn't think of precious precious Gertrude out there alone—in many weathers, in gray and shine, in snow and rain, in all those twenty years, never a day when her mind was far away. She lived: she rose, wishing she'd died when Baby did, wishing she too were under stone on that pitch in Père Lachaise, but there were things to be done, and the wish to be dead was lost in lonely living. She lived for another score of years, spoke, wrote, read, walked with Basket in the Luxembourg, went to the ballet, to *vernissages*, to Rome, to Spain, but always, on returning home, she knew she lived for the day she'd die. *Let it come*, she thought, *let it come*.

Some morning, they'd try to wake her, shake her, veined and meager, gently, but she'd have gone in the night, ticked her last and stopped, and there'd be no more widowed rounds to make, letters to write, journeys, talk, walks to take in the park, no more empty motion, and she'd lie there, quite still, and think: *This is the red-letter day.* Tomorrow they'd carry her coffin between banks of blooms that'd seem to have sprung from the street, and they'd pause at the parish church—*not for long*, she'd plead—and then they'd cross the wheel of Paris from rim to rim, and there they'd come to Baby's opened grave.

I will not tell her of the changes in our world: she would grieve. I will not say that Henri went a long while back, and Pablo's Olga, Hilda D., Marie. I will not tell her what became of our Fiesole (the well gone, the stifling stucco), I will be silent about the silence of Ernest (all those years!) and even the way he died: she would grieve. And I will make no mention of the pictures, taken away all: why should she grieve?

Into that grave the coffin would go, and then a dozen friends would pass, each letting a flower fall (*a dozen roses? would they be roses?*), and now a downpour of pebbles would start, bits of straw, minerals, a decompost of leaves, and old old Lutetian earth, ashes of the past, and slowly the sky would disappear, and in the dark she'd reach out for precious precious Gertrude, and Baby would kiss her hand.

Helen Keller, 1880–1968

THE THREE MONKEYS

I have been far away all this time, and I haven't left the room.
—Helen Keller, at 12

A fever at two left her bereft of her three best senses, and thereafter, being deaf, she heard no evil, and she saw no evil, being blind, but the wonder is why, on learning how to speak, she spoke no evil. Was there none in the world she dwelt in? Was space, black and silent, sinless too? Was there no hell to that Heaven? If so, she was pure as no one had been before her and no one since: evil never knew her.

In a picture taken at seven, she's shown in white on a dark ground, and, facing toward the right, she seems to be gazing at something outside the frame, at another child, it may be, or even that other world. In profile, she gives no sign of lacking vision; the eye seen looking off is seeing, and what it sees is beginning to cause a smile.

There are no standards within her head, no quantities, degrees, distances, colors, no ways of tracking time. All she owns is what she can feel through her skin, receive in the open arms of her mind—and who can say it is not enough? With her little, she may be making out great things in the night, and she's about to smile because she has measured immensities. One day she'd be learned in Latin, Greek, German, French, but still she'd speak no evil; she wouldn't know any.

Carlotta Monterey, 1888–1970

MRS. EUGENE O'NEILL

I have never had a home.
—Eugene O'Neill

A strange thing to say, she must've thought, she who'd made so many homes to hive him from the world, bought old ones where they stood or reared new ones from the ground, bought or built them in backwater and seagirt places, found them at land's end, put them where roads unraveled, on rocks, on sand, on other countries' hills. And still he'd said *I have never had a home*, and she must've wondered why, when homes were what she'd given him, changed to suit his fancy, arranged to fit his need. The stones she caused to be raised and those she tumbled down, the rooms added and the walls taken away, the variances she made with a glance, a sign—for whom were such if not for him?

176

I have never had a home, he'd said, and she hadn't understood the guilt, the red and shredding hands that tore him from within. She didn't know that he bled for the feud with his father and for a mother on morphine: such things were things of the past, she thought, and she must've been blind to color, because it never crossed her mind that he was bleeding on every page. *I have never had a home*, he'd said, but one was waiting, and he knew when he'd find it—the day he ran out of blood.

She didn't understand, she never would. To her, the blind one was he, or he'd've known that, all others failing, she herself was home for him, that within her he was safe from pang and peccadillo. She (it was so plain!), she was the small, secure, and private place that he'd been hunting all his life, she was his dim confessional, where he could be shriven without a priest. She didn't understand. She thought he wanted to live.

Eudora Welty, 1909–

THE NEIGHBORS

According to Algonquin traditions, the spirit-land was not far off, and roving hunters sometimes passed its confines unawares.

—Francis Parkman

Here too the dead and living mingle, well-bred shade with redneck clay, meet in Courthouse Square, the street, the store, stare at staring eyes and, on the rare occasion, pass the time of day. Here too, as in the Indian credenda, the compound world, the *comme il faut* and the crass, the blown and iridescent and the quick and kicking mass. Here too (where? in Yazoo City, in Tutwiler, Jackson, Okolona?) old warriors wander amid the new.

She writes, they all write, of the drift of life toward the daze of death, of suicides in rain-barrels, of failing hearts and slowly falling trees, trees that fall like leaves, she writes, they all write, of times past, of the Catastrophe, the blue flood that drowned the gray in black mud. She writes of now, she thinks, and so do they all, but now is only the near edge of then, and ghosts sometimes, and at times the living, roam across the border unawares.

Caresse Crosby, 1892–1970

I PROMISE YOU

that we shall die together.
                                          —Harry Crosby

We didn't, though, did we? You died forty years back, you and that Josephine, shot her through the head, and, two hours later, lying next to her in bed, shot yourself with that Belgian .25—you're forty years dead, and I'm alive. I've lived longer after your death than I lived before it, to no high purpose and no great gain, losing, really, losing more and more of what I began to lose that day behind that bedroom door. All I'm left with is your two-hour wait for the second shot, and I still weigh that pair of hours, still play them in my mind. Why the gap, I've always wondered, why the lifelong lapse of time? I know now that I'll never know: there's a door within the outer door, and the inner one is you.

How much you made of the sun! You spoke of it, wrote of it, had one tattooed on your back, but there was no sun in the lives we led, no core to our orderless motion: we simply spun in the dim of opium smoke, and all we ever saw was dire flora, parrot hues, tattoos of the sun, but fire never. We coupled with kindred couples in the Bois, we made the beast with lovers in the presence of our dogs, and once that I recall, you tried the sweet small favors of a boy. Champagne days and cocaine nights, whims that took us far, spilled us over France, sprees of buying when we bought, bought, until our home looked like the store. Life was money, we thought, and we spent every last cent on ourselves, but where in that dementia was the sun?

I promise you, you said, *that we shall die together*, but you died with Josephine, the six-months' bride of someone else. I think of the room where you were found, the broken-down door, the door inside that was you, and I wonder what you did during those two hours, wonder whether you sat or stood, stared from a window, read a book, straightened your tie, dwelt on the sun, on anything but death. . . . Was that it, Harry—after all that talk, did you have to make up your mind to die?

Auld Acquaintance (I. L.), 1910–70

A JUDAS WITH TITS

Verily I say unto you that one of you shall betray me.
Master, is it I?
                                                    —Matthew 26:21, 25

You spotted her from time to time, at some political session, it may have been, or in some eating-place, or maybe merely passing in the street. Only once, though, did you speak to her, or once that you recall, and what comes back of that occasion is the sense that she was using words to proffer herself. You gathered that in listening to her, in watching her, you weren't supposed to consider meaning, to respond to query or implication: you were to acknowledge *her*. That was her desire, to be herself recognized, and therefore she appeared to converse less in sound than gesture, and you can see her yet (in a hallway, was it, or at some meeting?), pressing her presence upon you, putting herself forward in the guise of speech. She may have held riches you were all unaware of, but she was stout and squat and more than somewhat plain, and you thought such treasure would hardly requite the search. Others doubtless thought the same, and her days and nights were spent alone.

The nights must've been bad. No one cared that she was growing older, going to waste, no one even knew she was there, sleepless in the dark with her fat delights, manipulating beatitude, fancying some coupled coming while coming by herself. Nor did she fare the better by day, at work, at play ungainly, at conclaves open and conclaves closed—there too she tendered her rareness, but the gift, neglected, was in effect refused.

Small wonder, then, that when summoned to bear witness against those who'd passed her by (in the hall, the street, the bed, the aisle), let her long and languish while they pleasured elsewhere, small wonder that she betrayed them one and all, swore each an enemy of the people, even as her teacher in the garden by the brook. Aye, small wonder that she sold their names by the dozen, and great were her rewards therefor, and never did she repent, as her mentor did, never she brought the silver back nor cast it on the ground.

And so the years went, the years went, and one night, quite unsought, her field of blood was found. Driving through a fog on a highway in Arizona, or was it near Jerusalem, she took the wrong way of the road (*Do not enter*, the sign had said), and a truck struck her, and she burst asunder, and her bowels gushed out, even as those of the other traitor, and much good may her silver do her, there where she has gone.

Marianne Moore, 1887–1972

THE ACCURACY OF THE VERNACULAR!

I scarcely think of any that comes into my so-called poems.

—Marianne Moore

Vernacular, from *verna*, bespeaking (does it not?) a slave born in his master's house, hence, in relation to language (this by extension, of course), native to the people of a particular place, an indigene. Odd, therefore, that you should think yourself free and clear of such ways of speech—and it *is* speech, your poetry, since so much of it seems to enter the ear, to be waves of sound, a master (a mistress) instructing slaves.

In your lines, meanings overlie, like the scales that tile your pangolin*—aye, let the pangolin reciprocate, let *it* describe *you*. You're armored too, cap-à-pie, imbricated, involucred with (as you say) "spruce-cone regularity." You overlap yourself, you wrap yourself in bracts of implication, a little of you showing in each, each the tip of something inner, a hinted invitation—come in, it not quite says, through this not quite open door.

*"The Pangolin," ll. 45–47: "The giant-pangolin-tail . . . tipped . . . with special skin." There are pangolins with a bare spot under the tip of the tail, used, it is thought, to palp for balance. But the giant pangolin (*Manis gigantea*) is entirely scaled; no skin is visible. *Encyclopedia Britannica*, 11th ed., vol. XX, p. 677c.

Aunt Jo, 1882–1972

THE PAINTED WOMAN

And how was the painted woman today, Julian?
—Aunt Rae

Aunt Jo, you called the other one, but she wasn't an aunt at all: she was your father's second wife. He married her when you were sixteen, while you were camping in Vermont, but by then you'd known her for a year or more, and your mind had been prepared for *the painted woman*—to Aunt Rae, your mother's sister, she was always *the painted woman*. A stepmother was bad enough, you'd been told, but this one was even worse: she was a divorcee with a daughter as old as your sister Ruth, and in ways he'd be unaware of, she'd beguile your father from his motherless own.

Her beauty was conceded. Of course she held your father's glance—the black plumes, the white skin, the silks she wore in décolleté (she bathed in milk!), how could she fail to turn his head? But she was false—*falsch*, Rae said—and her little elegancies, her seemly air, her fair words and *politesse*, all were sirenical, meant to gull her loveblind swain.

He wrote

Julian dear, I presume you have heard of my marriage— the event, in contemplation for some time, has been common gossip. I hope and trust, Julian, that this change in the life of your father will occasion no disappointment. . . .

and he wrote

I have taken an apartment on the Heights and the room allotted to you is one with a private bath. On your return from camp, there will be awaiting you a comfortable home, pleasant surroundings, and love and affection from me and my wife. In return, we expect very little, only honor and respect. . . .

and he wrote

Nothing you may do or say will make me lose the affection a father has for a son—except your loss of affection for me. Until then, there is nothing in the world that I am able to afford that you will not have. . . .

and he wrote

I do not have to tell you that my wife is entitled to your respect, and that as a dutiful son you will show it. If there is in your heart any antipathy toward her or me, I hope as you grow older, such prejudice will be eradicated. . . .

and he wrote

Your loving father.

You never saw that room of yours, never used the private bath, because you never entered the apartment on the

Heights where with *the painted woman* your father lived for the next nine years. By then, you were twenty-five (*as you grow older such prejudice, etc.*), and you had yet to fill his door. Nine years, and never that room knew you, never that private bath, and you wonder now whether you ever wondered about them, the color of the enamel, the tile, the rug, the curtains. But how could you not have wondered (loving son!), how could you not?

When you saw her again at last—what happened, what changed, what made you relent?—she was halfway through her forties, and some of her blaze and flaunt were gone, some of her power to daze the eye, but she was a stunner still with her still-black hair, her still-white skin (did she bathe in milk?). For some reason—what reason, for God's sake, and why so late?—you felt none of Rae's implanted hate (*And how was the painted woman today, Julian?*), and you saw her as someone come upon sad, and you knew that though you'd been swayed by another, her sadness had been made by you.

It wasn't the final marriage for either of them: with the years, distances. They died on different seaboards in the same year, she at ninety and he at ninety-four, but they arced time and miles to the end, dear to each other and dear to you. You were never able to tell her so, to say that the prejudice of *And how was the painted woman today, Julian?* had been eradicated, and you wish now that you had faith in contrition.

Unknown woman, Santa Barbara, 1970

THE WORD IS VERY NIGH UNTO THEE

You must've seen her often before you became aware of her, a fat old woman in green, and you knew then that she'd long been there at the wayside, like a tree, a street-sign, a certain stone, and in time, when you neared her beat, you found yourself looking ahead for a sight of her, and there she'd be on the grass margin of the road, a fat old woman in a straw poke and a pale green dress, the tree, the stone, the sign so long unseen.

In her hand, in the same hand always, it seemed, she carried a sheaf of tracts, the same sheaf, for all you knew, for she never gave them away. She held them before her, flowers to be had for the asking, but none of those she spoke to, bindlestiffs, girls, wandering Jews, minstrels on the bum, none showed a wish for, none requisitioned the Word.

She'd walk the strip of sward, clutching her unsought posies, limp, faded, soiled, and she'd talk with young and old, with those who heard and those whose minds were far away, with tethered dog and troubadour, with bold babies, staring at her straw hat, her green dress, and with many who lay asleep in the sun and sometimes in the rain. But none, with grace so nigh, none ever reached for her hand.

Josephine Baker, 1906(?)–75

CATCH A NIGGER BY THE TOE

When I'm in America all I have is bad luck.
                                        —Josephine Baker

> catch her in East St. Louis
> and after seventy years
> let her go
> set her free
> on a hillside back of Monaco

Her mother was a laundress, a chaser of dirt for the whites, and her father, name unknown, passed lightly over lower Illinois, a cloud that merely cast a shadow and soon was blown away, wherefore she might've been begotten of soap and steam, might've begun in some virgin bubble, a black immaculate sud. And yet she was the daughter of that drifting cloud, for she too was something in passage, a shimmering element, sequinned water, wind, and then she herself was gone in one last shivareen burst. From the hillside, the sea can be seen, a scatter of lights, a mobile reminder of Josephine.

> let her go
> let the nigger go

But first, shall mention be made of her chateau, of her cheetah, walked in the street on a leash, of her lavalliered monkey, her prince royal, and the sables that went with her skin . . . ?

                                                        No!

> let her go
> set her free
> on that hill in back of Monaco

185

Minnie Blumfield, 1886(?)–1977

WYANDOTTES, PLYMOUTH ROCKS

They're just chickens, but I love them.

—Minnie, "The Chicken Lady"

The poultry-truck was headed for the slaughterhouse when it struck a curb, a stone, a cross-bound car, and over-turned, spilling its freight across the highway. On striking the pavement, the crates burst, and a pell-mell of fowl fled the wreckage—red, yellow, barred with gray, they fled the tum-bril, escaped their headless fates. Oddly, though, flight took them only as far as the nearest perch, a post, a rail, a tree, and there they preened, picked at lice, piped the approach of Minnie, an Austrian Jew of eighty-three.

Many wars ago, sixty years and more, she herself had fled—widowed at Lemberg, was it?, or Yaroslavl, in the Car-pathians, along the Isonzo—and now hard by this road she dwelt alone and old, recalling at times the little that was left of dead-Jew Blumfield, the nothing, almost, for who but she knew these days that he'd ever been alive? She may have been thinking of him when she heard breaking wood, bird-gabble, beating wings.

The Wyandottes, the Plymouth Rocks, they picked and preened as Minnie neared, but none of them fled the old Jew-woman, for none feared her; instead, they merely seemed to listen as her skirts put aside the weeds. The rest is unknown. Did she pause below a branch, a wire, did she reach and stroke a Wyandotte, a Plymouth Rock, did she speak through one to all (in what tongue?), did she go among them, beck-oning, and did one and all come along?

They're just chickens, she said, *but I love them*, and for seven years she fed them, dosed them, sheltered them, con-versed with them, even, and therefore it may have been that Wyandottes, Plymouth Rocks, knew of her Jew, killed sixty years before—in Galicia, or was it far to the south, in Tyrol? Seven years did they preen and peck, the Wyandottes, the

186

Plymouth Rocks, and one day they became too much for old-Jew Minnie, and she was taken away to a Home, where for a while she may have ministered in her mind to chickens no longer there, and she may have been thinking of them, of Austria, of her dead husband, when she died at ninety-one.

Joan Crawford, 1908–77

A COAT OF ARCTIC FOX

I bought it because I felt low today.
—Joan Crawford

It was as if the words had come from within a cocoon, as if a great and growing pupa had spoken through its sheath, and at any moment, you thought, you'd see some imago emerge and fly or spring away. Instead, it was she who emerged. *I felt low*, she said from deep inside that pelt of hers, those ravened furs, and when she let the coat slide to the floor, she seemed to have skinned herself. *I felt low*, she said.

It's a small enough creature, the white fox, hardly the size of a median dog, and it lives, when alive, far to the north, where pink and green provinces fade to the pallor of the pole. There are no roads in that region, there are no trails across the marshes, and tracks are rare in the moss and snow: where seen, though, they lead to a pair of steel dentures, between which a fox died in a slush of blood. *I felt low*, she said after twenty-four such deaths in a sphagnum bog.

There are twenty-four skins in the coat that lies on the floor. There are twenty-four boreal foxes in that collar and skirt, those sleeves and raglan shoulders, there are twenty-four rings of blood around her feet. *Vulpes lagopus*, they used to be, living in the tenements of the rabbit, the burrows of the badger, feeding on sea-birds and lemmings and storing the latter for their young. Twenty-four white foxes, visible once only in the shadows they cast on the snow—they lie now in one-foot squares sewn together, a shucked white coat on the floor. *I felt low today*, she said.

Katherine Anne Porter, 1890(?)–

THE FOOLS FORGATHER AT VERA CRUZ

I am a passenger on that ship.
—Katherine Anne Porter

From a row of rooftops, the sun pours a salvo of light into the Plaza, white, smokeless, constant, like a snapshot of an execution. It finds its way through the sweet-by-night trees, pinks the blinds of dark arcades. The eyes of buzzards glow, and rounds of brass, and legends pulse on walls, as though the words were spelt in gas—*Pulque puro*, one such throbs, and *No anunciar*.

A few citizens sit in glares of linen, and between their sips of lemonade, they converse in glances, gestures, stillness, stares, speak in all but words. Silently they treat of an Indian asleep on a seat in the shade, of a lame and lurching beggar, of whores that pass in cotton and a higher class in gauze. They laze over limes, these loafers, and in tics and shrugs they phrase, in tappings on a table and clicks against a glass, and they deal, as they range the balconies, with a gray cat, a parrot, a chained monkey, a dog that has the mange.

And then they rise, the linened citizens, and stroll toward the end of life in the middle of a printed page. The waiters survive them for a paragraph or two, cursing gainlessly, as at sweat, when the fools begin to arrive. They too are exudations, the weepage of trains, rooms, cantinas, motorcars, they seem to seep into view, to flow across the Square. There are Switzers on this drift, and a bride and groom Mex, and there are priests, a pair on tour, and a squarehead Swede is seen, and a strolling-player troupe, and a slew of Dutchmen, one a traveler in canonicals, a merchandising Jew—and, smoke

188

from Havana, the steerage smell of Spics deported, eight hundred and seventy-six in all, ballast for the *Vera* on this crossing of the Styx.

I am a passenger on that ship, she says. I go hand in hand with Mann and Frau, I pet the dog Bebe. I dance with gypsy dancers, I chat with La Condesa, lady *déclassée*, and that is I, next to the wedded lovers, I nodding to the Jew, I discussing dogma with the priests. I walk the decks with singers, painters, medicos from Cuba, and Glocken the kyphotic freak. I talk to innkeepers, dying healers, officers, I put Bebe through his bag of bulldog tricks. *I am a passenger on that ship*, she says, I'm even in the hold with those excretory Spics. They're headed for hell, she says, and when they sail, I'll sail too. I sidle with the hunchback, beg with the dog, sell birettas with the Dusseldorf Jew. I am they, shopworn, vile, and quick to anger; I am they, gluttonous, lustful, led by the nose like Bebe. *I am a passenger on that ship.* . . .

You one of the fools? Cool coiled lady, quiet, sudden, and serpentine—you one of the fools? Nay, lady, you're merely here to see them off.

Georgia O'Keeffe, 1887–

I
A PAINTING CALLED *WHITE BARN, NO. 1*

It's all right, if you like barns.
                                    —Nathanael West

And then he walked away to other things, to the jagged Marins, maybe, or to the soft, the round, the almost edible Demuths, and you were left with a white wall, a black roof, and bands of grass and sky—*if you like barns*, he'd said, and he was in another part of the room, among the jackstraw Marins, the ready-to-pick Demuths. He's been a long while dead, and his spoken words are mostly lost, but now and then a phrase replays itself in your head, and the sound summons a

189

time gone by and a bygone place, and for a moment the time is now and the place here, and again he's saying *If you like barns*, and again he walks away.

The phrase would come back to you every time you saw that picture or saw it reproduced. *If you like barns*, you'd think, and you'd seem to hear a dead man speak in some gallery of your mind. He'd speak too when you stood before other pictures or leafed them in a book, pelvises, antlers, skulls in the sand, and *if you like barns* became *if you like bones*, and it changed as well for great and growing crosses, like dangers in a dream, for roads that kept on paying out, as pennants did in the wind, for clam-shells open and clam-shells shut, for flower genitalia and the privities of hills.

But in the end, it wasn't his gang-hooked dig that turned her pictures into paint. It was the pictures themselves: they were dry water, you thought, heat that wasn't hot. The barn was empty, you came to realize, or, worse than empty, it had never been a barn. The black doors, if doors they were, gave on no dim and steamed interior where stock had ever stood and pissed on straw: they were holes between a bright void and a dark one, and you seemed to be peering from nil through naught at nothing.

If you like barns, dead Pep had said, but had he known, you wondered, that she'd painted no barns at all, that she'd merely colored space? Had he known that her roads had never been ridden on, that her birds had never flown? Had he missed presences in those pictures, people, had he sensed that the labia of her flowers were too cold to be kissed? *If you like barns*—you can hear his voice, you can see the picture yet, and both of them are dead.

II
PHOTOGRAPHS OF A PAINTER*

. . . terrible winds and a wonderful emptiness
—Georgia O'Keeffe

a: bust
Her hand, rather like a fanned-out wing, lies be-

190

tween her bare breasts. The nipples are low in brilliance, almost as pale as the studded rings around them.

b: torso

Her arms are raised in a pose that drains her thin breasts thinner, half-draws them back within her body, shows the bones that she contains, and her thighs collide in a fog of hair.

c: hand

A dark coat-sleeve uncouples it at the wrist, and quite whole but wholly apart, it's poised between two bright buttons and pointing at her heart.

d: face

It seems to depend from something above and outside the frame, to extend dark-skinned downward into a black deep, a shape like India.

e: full figure

At the corner of a porch, a downspout bends into a bed of begonias, and nearby, on a doormat, she sits beside a sketchbook, a tin of water colors, and a glass of colored water. She wears a homemade sweater, a white dress, and high shoes laced, and a hand, that outspread wing, curves across her skirt. Her face is lifted a little and slightly turned, and she's looking past you at a tree, a cloud, the blue of the sky, or simply space.

No one knows how many pictures he took of her, some say five hundred, some say more, but whatever the number, they mark the house she lives in, the particular shape and size, the proportions, the style, but the blinds are drawn on the eyes, and they give no view inside. Five hundred pictures of the same house, pictures taken in all weathers and all degrees of light, taken in whole and taken in detail, five hundred pictures of a house and never a one of the door. *A wonderful emptiness*, she said of the desert, but she must've meant the world.

*By Alfred Stieglitz.

191

Agnes von Kurowsky, 1892–

IN THE LATE SUMMER OF THAT YEAR

Miss Barkley was quite tall. She wore a nurse's uniform, was blonde and had a tawny skin and gray eyes. I thought she was very beautiful.

—Ernest Hemingway

The real and the written, he thought, and they seemed to have mingled, like smoke from a cigarette, blue at one end and brown at the other, and they were entwined now in a color neither blue nor brown but both, and the compound drifted through his mind, *the real and the written*, and he could not break it down, make fact and fiction clear. Nothing was clear these days, the days themselves blurred at the edges, bled, and when he recalled a word he supposed he'd heard, it might've been one he'd read.

She was very beautiful, he thought, *blonde, tawny skin, gray eyes*, but was he thinking of the one who'd seen to him at the Ospedale in Milano, the one who'd bathed him clean of the trainride, given him a cocktail, an eggnog, a dose of castor oil, the one he'd kissed, held close, loved for the way she shook him with the beating of her heart? Or was he gone on some creation of his own, a spelled-out dream, an œuvre that spoke his speeches, saying *you mustn't you're not well enough you're not strong enough you can't you shouldn't . . . that was just madness?* Which of the two? he thought— or, now in the late summer of a later year, were the real and the written one?

He looked about him at the gear he'd spent his life with, the watchmaker-work of reel and rifle, at sights, lures, and agate guides, at steel, leather, wood, glass, at a machine for making words, and he wondered why they moved him so little, less than his convoluted memories of a time nearly lost in time that had passed. *I'll say just what you wish and I'll do what you wish and then you will never want any other girls. I'll do what you want and say what you want. I'll be a great success.*

192

She was a fine girl, he thought, but he couldn't remember which girl he was thinking of, the one who'd so professed in a book, or the one who'd fed him, dressed him, changed his bed, but never so spoken at all. Of one of them he'd said or set down *We had a lovely time that summer*, and he tried to remember the one it was, because that one he'd loved, and he loved her yet, the real Agnes or the written Catherine. The real or the written, which?, he wondered as he went with the gun to the entry hall. . . .

Eleanor Roosevelt, 1884–1962

AMONG THE ROSES

(From the will of Franklin D. Roosevelt: " . . . a plain white marble monument, no carving or decoration, no device or inscription, except on the south side . . . It is my hope that my dear wife will on her death be buried there also.")

I was one of those who served his purposes.

—Eleanor Roosevelt

When they quarried and cut the stone, she thought, it would be brought here to head the grave, and on its south face, as the will provided, someone would chase their names, his with the dates of birth and death, hers as yet with one. She tried to read ahead to the missing year, to see herself dead, an occupant of the room next door, but tomorrow was cast in a haze of remembered things, and it was the past she saw, not the days to come.

In her mind, pages turned back to a photo of a child in a white dress and a wide black sash, a bucktoothed and chinless child clutching a toy dog hung with two tin bells that still thinly seemed to ring. And there were other pictures, some with her impassive mother and her randandy father, both soon gone, and there were pets, picnics, boats, classmates on a lawn, and then came a sped-up series of weddings, hackneys, brownstone fronts, hats like aeries, fifth cousins once removed, and a pose, taken in a gondola, that showed her holding her husband's boater—and they were all beginning to blur when one of them stopped the machine. It was a beach scene, and in it a young woman in a white dress and a wide black sash waded through the train of a wave; the figure faced away, and hiked skirts bared comely legs to the knees, and she stared, as Franklin may have done that day, and she wondered when she'd ceased to please him.

She rummaged for a reason. What phrase had offended, what silence when she should have spoken, what gown had been wrong, what color off, what error of taste had she made, what truth told, what dispassion shown when heat was called for, what had she given or refused, what done or not done, what duties had she enjoyed too much and what pleasures had left her cold, what had cooled him, what awkward gesture had he caught, what light had revealed her plainness and hidden her sightly eyes?

And now a mutoscope of pictures, stills wheeled by memory, and she saw streets and styles change by the moment, she saw people age and die, and armies and armadas passed, and birds flew in strange formation, and she heard guns in the distance and the tin bells on a toy dog, but nothing at all from the adjoining room.

Alice Roosevelt Longworth, 1884–1980

WITH HER FEET UP ON THE HANDLEBARS

*I know, Alice, that you don't mean to be disagreeable, but
you don't somehow seem to be very nice.*
                                                —Eleanor Roosevelt

In her view, Eleanor was a ninny, an opinion she'd hold
to the end of her life. She thought her cousin gauche at best,
ill at ease, joyless, badly dressed: it was a far cry from eleanor-
brown to alice-blue, and further still were the tinctures of
their minds. Fancy Eleanor smoking on the White House
roof, fancy her cycling the streets of Washington and showing
the world her drawers! Alice smoked, of course, and she
spoke of men and what they did with whores, and when
Eleanor said *No one should talk about things like that*, Alice
laughed, drew deep on a Turkish Trophy, and blew gray
clouds at the prude. The ninny, she may have thought, the
ugly duckling. . . .

The swan was Alice, and who was unaware of her Mansion years, of the style in which she piled her hair, who hadn't
heard of the gowns she wore at galas, the sleigh-rides in the
dark, hadn't read of her junket to Japan with Nick (what a
lark, those races in a rickshaw!), who knew naught of four-in-
hands up Fifth and spanking rounds of the park? The charades
and other games she played, the waltzes under crystal, the
Mumm's and masquerades—who hadn't wined and whirled
with her through endless nights and days?

It came as a shock, therefore, when the endless ended.
An overthrow, it seemed to Alice, a subversion of their betters
by the worse, and if she shivered as with a chill, it was because she heard the click of needles from a still far-off defarge.
There'd be no more jade from China's empress, no more gold
brocade, and the Gobelins would cease to flow from France.
On the air now rode upstart names, and there were later
crazes, newer ways of doing hair, other games were being
learned, and a bluer blue than alice was the rage.

195

And so the years passed, and the faces changed, and though she yearned for the reign she'd lost, sought it through her father and for the last time through her Nick, it returned never. Instead, the ninny came, occupied *her* house, greeted *her* guests, took *her* place . . . ! She fixed her for that, Alice did. She let Franklin tryst with Lucy under her venereal roof. Oh, she fixed that Eleanor, all right!

Sara Delano Roosevelt, 1854–1941

JUST THE SWEETEST DEAREST MAMA

Some day I hope that she will love me.
　　　　　　　　　　—Eleanor Roosevelt

But there was no love for her in sweetest dearest Mama, and through the sweet dear screen of her face, that lack of love could be seen, the inscriptions of pride, resentment, scorn, and arrogation, the cut-glass mouth, the eyes that were worn like tinted lenses. At twenty-six, she'd married a Hudson River squire, a widower twice her age, and with his fargone fire and her water-ice blood, it was a marvel that his seed survived the chill, the dark, the glutinous gurges of the swim upstream. It did more: it throve there where swimming ended, and in time it became something to be ejected with the same disgust that attended its conception—in a spate of amniotic slush, it became a son.

Her duty now done, she was free to turn to the squire-to-be, a less lickerish lover, and with him there were no lunging invasions, no cataclysms of gism to wash away. He loved as through a mirror, touching now and then with fingertips, penetrating never. Ah, what years she gave him—years of pony-carts and philately, sailboats, guns, birds stuffed and on the wing—until *she* came, saying *Some day I hope that she will love me!*

Golda Meir, 1898–1979

A VOYAGE TO PALESTINE, 1921

What in the world do you expect to find in Palestine?
—British immigration inspector

Zion, she might've said, but what could she have added
to make him understand? Could she have spoken of her birth
in Kiev, of the massacres in Pinsk, could she have told him of
Old World fears and hunger, of hope deferred in the New—
would such things have made him understand what had to be
found in this sand and these stones of Palestine, in these
browned and quivering hills? *Zion,* she might've said. *Being
one of its haughty daughters, I expect to find Zion,* but he'd
never have understood. How could he, when it was less than
clear to her?

She herself could not have known that there was more
for her here than in the *Goldene Medineh,* more in this sand
and stone than in the golden land she'd left. She could barely
see it for the glare, the shimmer, but it was there, sunstruck
or in the black shade, it was in eyes that stared through rims
of flies, in blind beggars and their meager dogs, and there was
something about the olives, willowy in the hot wind, about
those stiff and grasping figs. . . .

What in the world do you expect to find in Palestine? the
inspector asked her, and she gazed at the high and heavy
sky—zion-blue, she may have thought—and in that moment,
she may have known, knew!, what had brought her here in
the *S. S. Pokahontas,* fifty-four days on the way from Boston.
This was no wilderness seen from the top of Pisgah; it was
the goodly country down below! *What do you expect to find
. . . ?* the man said, but how could she tell him that the lost
had been found? He wouldn't understand.

Marguerite Sanford 1905–

DEDICATION PAGE

You've never written me a love-letter.

—Maggie

But it has all been a love-letter. . . .